DAD'S ARMY

THE DEADLY ATTACHMENT
MUM'S ARMY
THE GODIVA AFFAIR
THE FLORAL DANCE

by Jimmy Perry and David Croft

SAMUEL FRENCH

samuelfrench.co.uk

For Amateur Production Enquiries

United Kingdom and World
excluding north america
plays@samuelfrench.co.uk
020 7255 4302/01

Each title is subject to availability from Samuel French, depending upon country of performance.

THINKING ABOUT PERFORMING A SHOW?

There are thousands of plays and musicals available to perform from Samuel French right now, and applying for a licence is easier and more affordable than you might think

From classic plays to brand new musicals, from monologues to epic dramas, there are shows for everyone.

Plays and musicals are protected by copyright law, so if you want to perform them, the first thing you'll need is a licence. This simple process helps support the playwright by ensuring they get paid for their work and means that you'll have the documents you need to stage the show in public.

Not all our shows are available to perform all the time, so it's important to check and apply for a licence before you start rehearsals or commit to doing the show.

LEARN MORE & FIND THOUSANDS OF SHOWS

Browse our full range of plays and musicals, and find out more about how to license a show
www.samuelfrench.co.uk/perform

Talk to the friendly experts in our Licensing team for advice on choosing a show and help with licensing
plays@samuelfrench.co.uk   020 7387 9373

Acting Editions

BORN TO PERFORM

Playscripts designed from the ground up to work the way you do in rehearsal, performance and study

---

Larger, clearer text for easier reading

Wider margins for notes

Performance features such as character and props lists, sound and lighting cues, and more

---

+ CHOOSE A SIZE AND STYLE TO SUIT YOU

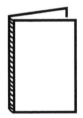

STANDARD EDITION

Our regular paperback book at our regular size

SPIRAL-BOUND EDITION

The same size as the Standard Edition, but with a sturdy, easy-to-fold, easy-to-hold spiral-bound spine

LARGE EDITION

A4 size and spiral bound, with larger text and a blank page for notes opposite every page of text – perfect for technical and directing use

---

LEARN MORE | samuelfrench.co.uk/actingeditions

**Other plays by DAVID CROFT
(written with JEREMY LLOYD)
published by Samuel French**

'Allo 'Allo

Are You Being Served?

**FIND PERFECT PLAYS TO PERFORM AT
www.samuelfrench.co.uk/perform**

AUTHOR'S NOTE

Dad's Army has been through many stages in its lifetime. Apart from the television series of which there were 80 episodes—two of them of an hour's duration—there was a film, a long-running series of radio shows and a London stage production at The Shaftesbury Theatre.

When compiling the London stage version we were keen not to include incidents and sketches that had been seen on television and as a result we concocted what we described on the posters as "A Nostalgic Music and Laughter Show of Britain's Finest Hour". This worked out wonderfully at that time but it was many years ago. Nostalgia is not what it used to be. Many of the household names in wartime showbusiness are unknown to present day audiences.

As a result, when assembling a show for amateur societies we thought a different approach was needed. We thought that societies are now keen to perform episodes that have been seen on television and to give impersonations of the well-loved characters. The other consideration was to allow for the fact that there is usually a preponderance of females in most societies so we have included episodes where they are well represented. If extra time is needed we have left it to societies to judge the age of their audiences and include such wartime songs as they think suitable. They can thus exploit the musical talent in their midst. We know there is a lot of producing talent out there. Go to it!

David Croft
2004

When I saw the first two productions of *Dad's Army* by amateur dramatic societies I was amazed to see how everything came together; scripts that were written for television worked so well on the stage. Then the thought struck me—how the Home Guard and amateur dramatic societies had so much in common; it's a rather absurd comparison but they were both made up of members of the local community, and both did their legitimate jobs by day and went on duty at night! The Home Guard ceased to exist nearly 60 years ago but the amateur dramatic societies go from strength to strength and they are something uniquely British.

Dad's Army can be staged as simply or ambitiously as each society wishes. The church hall can be a full set or just tabs with a few pieces of scenery. To cover scene changes there are so many wonderful wartime songs that can be performed on the front tabs. Rifles and uniforms can be hired from various sources—a trawl of the Internet can yield hundreds of outlets. Videos of the televised episodes are readily available for business that may not be included in the original scripts. Having said that, feel free to interpret the scripts in your own way. You will find the characters rich, round and a joy to play.

Jimmy Perry
2004

DAD'S ARMY

*We have included "The Floral Dance" sketch because it was so successful in the production at The Shaftesbury Theatre, London, and was also performed by the *Dad's Army* team when they appeared in the Royal Command Variety Performance. If the length of the entertainment permits, it makes a wonderful finish to the first or second half of the show and includes a larger cast of Wardens and Ladies.

J.P. and D.C.

THE DEADLY ATTACHMENT

THE DEADLY ATTACHMENT

Original television transmission by the BBC on 31st October, 1973 with the following cast of characters:

CAPTAIN MAINWARING	Arthur Lowe
SERGEANT WILSON	John Le Mesurier
LANCE CORPORAL JONES	Clive Dunn
PRIVATE FRAZER	John Laurie
PRIVATE WALKER	James Beck
PRIVATE GODFREY	Arnold Ridley
PRIVATE PIKE	Ian Lavender
U-BOAT CAPTAIN	Philip Madoc
CHIEF WARDEN HODGES	Bill Pertwee
VERGER	Edward Sinclair
COLONEL	Robert Raglan
PRIVATE SPONGE	Colin Bean
PLATOON	Desmond Callum-Jones, George Hancock Evan Ross, Leslie Noyes, William Gossling, Freddie White, Freddie Wiles, Roger Bourne, Michael Moore
POLICEMAN	Ray Emmins
NAZI SAILORS	Les Conrad, Reg Turner, Clive Roger, Danny Lions, Alan Thomas, Emmett Hennessy, Barry Summerford

CHARACTERS

CAPTAIN MAINWARING
SERGEANT WILSON
LANCE CORPORAL JONES
PRIVATE FRAZER
PRIVATE GODFREY
PRIVATE WALKER
PRIVATE PIKE
PRIVATE SPONGE
PRIVATE HANCOCK
COLONEL
U-BOAT CAPTAIN
CHIEF WARDEN HODGES, ARP Warden
MR YEATMAN, the Verger
Other members of the PLATOON and seven U-BOAT SAILORS

The action takes place in the church hall and office at Walmington-on-Sea on the south coast of England

Time—1940

Scene One

The Church Hall.

The lights come up on a tableau: the platoon in heroic pose. Above them is a scroll sign with the words "Walmington-on-Sea Home Guard". Hold the tableau for applause.

The platoon form up in two ranks at attention. **PIKE** *is wearing a woolly scarf over his uniform.*

MAINWARING Walmington-on-Sea Home Guard, slope arms. Forward march.

The platoon march right downstage.

Platoon, halt. Salute. Order arms.

JONES *is a beat behind.*

Stand at ease. Attention.

JONES *is a beat behind.*

Try and keep up, Jones.

JONES Sorry, sir. I'm not myself today. You see my brawn went runny, and you can't slice runny brawn, sir.

MAINWARING All right, Jones.

JONES You have to serve it by the spoonful, and then you can't wrap it, it drips through the paper.

MAINWARING That will do, Jones. Now pay attention, men. Now I'm going to inspect the men, Wilson. Call them to attention.

WILSON Rightho. Attention!

MAINWARING Not like some nancy boy. You're supposed to be a sergeant. Bark it out.

WILSON *(barking)* Attention!

JONES Permission to speak, sir. I have to inform you that we are already at attention.

WILSON So you are. Stand at ease.

The men stand at ease. JONES *is a beat behind.*

JONES I wasn't ready then. You caught me on the hop.

MAINWARING Attention! *(He inspects* JONES*)* Very smart, Jones.

JONES Thank you, sir. I am also very alert. Even as I am talking to you, my eyes are everywhere. Whoa! *(He grabs* PIKE*'s throat)*

PIKE What are you doing, Mr Jones?

JONES You moved. He moved, sir. And my reflex action came into play instantly.

PIKE Can I stand somewhere else, please Mr Mainwaring?

MAINWARING Stay where you are, Pike. How many times have I told you, Pike, not to wear that scarf on parade?

PIKE My mum makes me wear it. I've got a weak chest. You ask Uncle Arthur.

MAINWARING Wilson. *(He takes him downstage)* That boy's mother pampers and spoils him to death. Can't you do anything about it?

WILSON Not really, sir. You see Mavis, I mean Mrs Pike, makes him wear a scarf because he gets croup.

MAINWARING Croup? That's what chickens get.

WILSON He gets it as well.

MAINWARING Extraordinary! *(He passes on to* FRAZER*)*

FRAZER Captain Mainwaring, may I point out that while you're walking up and down wasting time, the Germans are just across the channel waiting to invade us.

MAINWARING Thank you, Frazer. I've made arrangements, Frazer. *(He passes on to* **WALKER***)* Very smart, Walker. *(He taps him on the chest)* Just a minute. What's that?

WALKER *(pulling a flat half bottle of whisky out of his blouse)* A bottle of whisky.

MAINWARING How many times have I told you not to bring your black market activities on parade. Get rid of that bottle.

WALKER *(to the man next to him)* It's up to him. He ordered it.

MAINWARING What? Well... I'll overlook it this time. *(He passes on to* **GODFREY***)*

GODFREY Good-evening.

MAINWARING Good-evening? This isn't a church social, Godfrey. This is war—and take that smile off your face. I am carrying out a military inspection.

GODFREY Do you think you'll be long, sir?

MAINWARING Why do you ask?

GODFREY Well I'd rather like to...

MAINWARING You'll just have to wait. Stand at ease. *(He crosses back to* **WILSON***)* Now pay attention men. I have just received a new directive from GHQ regarding Nazi parachutists, and I'll read it to you. *(Reading)* "There is a danger that the Home Guard might confuse British pilots and air crews who are bailing out, with actual German parachute troops". *(Pause)* Not that our chaps get shot down very often, of course, but this could happen. *(Pause)* "A good point to remember here is the fact that no British plane contains more than six men. *(Pause)* So if you see a bunch of parachutists floating down, you count them, *(pause)* and if there are more than six, you shoot them in the air."

PIKE Mr Mainwaring.

MAINWARING Yes.

PIKE Mr Mainwaring, if they're dressed as nuns, do we still count them?

MAINWARING You count them however they're dressed, although it isn't likely that a whole plane-load of real nuns would drop by parachute.

JONES You never know, sir. I look at it this way. Supposing somewhere in occupied France there is a nunnery. And one day the chief nun calls all the other nuns together and she says, "Now listen, girls, I've had enough of being under Nazi heels, let us escape to dear old England", and they all creep out and steal a plane. And they fly, and fly and fly. And when these flying nuns get here, they don't know how to land, so they all jump out in parachutes.

MAINWARING I think you're getting into the realms of fantasy now, Jones.

JONES But it is a possibility, sir. It is a possibility.

MAINWARING It's a million to one chance. But I suppose we should take every precaution.

WILSON Excuse me, sir. If I may be allowed to interject at this point of the discussion?

MAINWARING Hmmmm?

WILSON It's really perfectly simple, you see. As they float down, the turbulence of the air will cause the habits to rise, and we shall be able to see their legs. Then we can tell if they're real nuns or not.

MAINWARING A very good point, Wilson, very good. You must look at their legs.

GODFREY Mr Mainwaring, *(pause)* I'm afraid I don't think I should care to look at nuns' legs, sir. It would be very impolite.

MAINWARING You'd just have to force yourself, Godfrey. This is war.

PIKE Mr Mainwaring, I don't know what real nuns' legs look like. I've never seen them.

WALKER If it comes to that, I don't think anybody has.

FRAZER Hairy 'uns!

MAINWARING I beg your pardon, Frazer?

FRAZER If they're Nazis, they'll have nasty hairy legs with jackboots on.

WALKER What do we do if the real nuns have got nasty hairy legs with jackboots on?

MAINWARING That will do, Walker. Now. *(Reading)* "If a Nazi parachutist was floating down with his hands up, would you think this was strange?"

WALKER Not half as strange as if he was floating up with his hands down.

MAINWARING I shan't tell you again, Walker. If he is floating down with his hands up, this does not necessarily mean that he is surrendering. He could have a grenade concealed in each hand, so watch it.

The phone rings in the office.

Answer the phone, Pike.

PIKE Yes, Mr Mainwaring.

PIKE *crosses to the office.*

MAINWARING By the way, Wilson, while we are on the subject of grenades, have you primed our stock of Mills bombs?

WILSON No, sir.

MAINWARING I told you to do it yesterday.

WILSON But it's awfully dangerous, sir.

MAINWARING War is awfully dangerous, Wilson. What would you do if a hoard of Nazi parachutists were to descend on the Church Hall? Say "Wait a minute while we prime our grenades?" I want those bombs ready for instant use. See to it tonight.

WILSON Yes, sir.

PIKE *returns.*

PIKE You're wanted on the phone, Mr Mainwaring. GHQ, it's very urgent.

MAINWARING Of course. *(He crosses to the door)* Take over, Wilson.

MAINWARING *and* **PIKE** *jostle through the office door.*

MAINWARING Get out of the way, boy! And shut the door.

PIKE Yes, sir. *(He shuts the door, remaining in the office)*

MAINWARING From the other side.

PIKE Well you should've said. *(He sulks off into the hall, shutting the door behind him)*

MAINWARING *(picking up the phone)* Stupid boy!

The lights come up on the **COLONEL** *on the phone, sitting at his desk.*

COLONEL What was that, Mainwaring?

MAINWARING Nothing, sir, you wanted me?

COLONEL Yes, Mainwaring. I've got a very important job for you to do.

MAINWARING Excellent. What is it?

COLONEL I've just had a message from the police. A fishing boat has picked up a U-Boat captain and seven members of the crew. They're down at the harbour now, locked in the ship's hold.

MAINWARING By Jove, that's good news.

COLONEL I want you to pick them up and take them back to the church hall. I'll send an armed escort over to collect them.

MAINWARING Face to face with the enemy at last, eh, sir? Don't worry, we'll take good care of them.

COLONEL They won't give you much trouble. They've been drifting at sea for two days in a rubber dinghy. Good luck.

MAINWARING Thank you, sir.

The lights go down on the COLONEL.

MAINWARING *hangs up, strides to the door and opens it.*

Good news, men! After all these months of waiting, we're finally going to get to grips with the enemy.

WALKER *(to* JONES*)* Blimey, don't tell me we're going to invade France.

WILSON *hurries over to* MAINWARING.

WILSON You're not going to do anything too hasty, are you, sir?

MAINWARING I've got something very important to say to the men.

WILSON Have you found out what nuns' legs look like?

MAINWARING All right, Wilson. *(To the men)* A fishing boat has picked up a U-Boat crew, and we're going down to the harbour to collect them.

JONES Fix bayonets! We're going to collect a U-Boat crew. Fix bayonets! *(He rushes over to* MAINWARING, *waving his rifle with bayonet fixed)* I can't wait to get at 'em, Mr Mainwaring, I just can't wait.

MAINWARING Put that bayonet away, Jones. There's plenty of time for that when we get there.

JONES I can't help it, sir. When I get a whiff of action, I reach for my bayonet. It's a second nature, I tell you, second nature.

MAINWARING Fall the men in outside.

JONES Yes sir, yes sir. Fall in outside to collect a U-Boat crew. Rifles and bayonets at the double.

JONES *starts to hustle the men out.*

MAINWARING Wilson! Pike! Wilson, while we're gone, I want you and Pike to prime all the grenades.

WILSON If you insist, sir.

MAINWARING I want it done by the time I get back. Right men, get a move on.

MAINWARING *follows the men out.*

The lights fade as they exit. Music.

Scene Two

In the office. A little later that evening.

The music fades out as the lights come up in the office on WILSON *by the desk and* PIKE *in the doorway with a bomb in his hand. There are some Mills bombs laid out on the desk.*

PIKE OK, youse guys, dis is a showdown. Share this pineapple amongst you! *(He pretends to pull the pin with his teeth and bowl the bomb through the door)*

WILSON For goodness' sake, put that down, Frank.

PIKE Those Chicago gangsters used to call them pineapples, Uncle Arthur. I saw it in that film *Scarface* with Paul Muni.

WILSON I don't care what they called them, they're very dangerous.

PIKE These are quite safe, they haven't got detonators in. *(He holds it up to his eye)* Look you can see right through. Shall I get them? *(He goes to move)*

WILSON Stay where you are, Frank, and don't do anything. I'll get the detonators. *(He crosses to the cupboard and gingerly takes out a box)* This is so risky. *(He opens the box. Pause)* There's only two in this box!

PIKE *(lurching enthusiastically towards the cupboard)* There's some more boxes at the back of the cupboard. Shall I—

WILSON *(fending him off)* I don't want you to touch them, Frank. *(He pulls a box from the back of the cupboard and looks at the label)* Hmmm! *(Reading)* "Dummy primers for training purposes only".

PIKE We don't want dummy detonators, they're no good. There's a box of real ones at the back.

PIKE *lurches for the cupboard again,* WILSON *stops him.*

WILSON Wait a minute, Frank. Look, er...um, how would it be if we were to put these dummies in the grenades, instead of the real thing.

PIKE But Mr Mainwaring said we had to have them ready for instant action. What would we do if the Germans came along?

WILSON We could soon change them round, it wouldn't take a moment. I mean we could get it done before the bells had stopped ringing.

PIKE Mr Mainwaring will be awfully cross if he finds out.

WILSON Yes, but I can't help feeling he'll be even more cross if we all get blown up, now come on let's do that.

They move to the desk and begin putting detonators in the bombs.

Blackout.

Scene Three

The Church Hall. Later that evening.

MAINWARING, WALKER, FRAZER *and* GODFREY *enter,*
followed by the U-BOAT CAPTAIN *and* SEVEN SAILORS.
The rest of the platoon bring up the rear with fixed
bayonets. JONES *is milling around waving his bayonet*
at the prisoners, who have their hands on their heads.

JONES Left, right, left, right. *(As they enter) Hande Hoch! Hande*
Hoch! Keep those Handeys Hock!

MAINWARING All right, Jones. They can put their hands down.

JONES Right. Handeys down! Handeys down! Nix Hock! *(He*
gestures with his rifle)

MAINWARING What are you doing, Jones?

JONES They're still hocking, sir!

MAINWARING Never mind that. Now, Frazer, get the Lewis
gun and set it up on the stage, so that it has a clear sweep
of the entire hall.

FRAZER Ay, ay, sir.

FRAZER *goes into the office.*

MAINWARING Sponge! Hancock!

SPONGE
HANCOCK } *(together)* Sir!

MAINWARING Go and get a stepladder.

SPONGE Right you are, Mr Mainwaring.

SPONGE *and* HANCOCK *exit.*

MAINWARING Corporal Jones!

JONES Yes, sir.

MAINWARING Get those prisoners into a tight huddle in the middle of the hall.

JONES Yes, sir. *(To the prisoners)* At the double in a tight huddle. In a small group in the middle of the hall. Move! Come along now.

JONES *and the rest of the platoon push the prisoners into a tight group in the middle of the hall.* WILSON *comes out of the office, followed by* PIKE.

WILSON *(entering through the office door)* You got back then, sir. Did they give you any trouble?

MAINWARING Not really. *(Lowering his voice)* But they're an ugly mob. You see that captain, you want to watch him, he's a surly brute. He's done nothing else but sneer and smoke cigarettes.

WILSON That reminds me, sir, I wonder if he's got any left. I seem to have run out.

MAINWARING This isn't a cocktail party, Wilson. Did you prime those grenades?

PIKE Well, Mr Mainwaring, we—

WILSON I think I can honestly say, sir, that all the grenades now have detonators in them.

At this point GODFREY *makes himself comfortable in a chair by the stage and slowly nods off to sleep unnoticed during the following.*

MAINWARING Good. Pike, get the Tommy gun.

PIKE *(with disbelief)* The Tommy gun!

MAINWARING The Tommy gun.

PIKE Thank you! Yes, Mr Mainwaring.

PIKE *goes into the office.* JONES *comes over to* MAINWARING *and* WILSON.

JONES The prisoners are now in a huddle in the middle of the hall, sir.

MAINWARING Thank you, Jones.

WALKER *(to one of the* **SAILORS***)* 'Ere listen. Tell your mates that I am in the market for purchasing Nazi daggers, swastikas, badges, signed pictures of Hitler or similar souvenirs. I'll give you a good price.

The Sailor shakes his head.

Oh blimey, you don't speak English, do you? Look, Nazi daggers, see daggers.

WALKER *makes a stabbing motion at the sailor, who jumps back. The* **CAPTAIN** *crosses to* **WALKER.**

CAPTAIN Get away from my men at once.

WALKER Don't start on me, mate.

MAINWARING Come over here, Walker.

WALKER *crosses to* **MAINWARING, WILSON** *and* **JONES,** *who are standing in a tight group away from the prisoners.*

How dare you fraternize with the enemy.

WALKER I was only asking them if there was anything they needed.

MAINWARING I'll attend to that. *(Lowering his voice)* Now listen. The armed escort will be here shortly to collect these prisoners. Meanwhile we want maximum security, Wilson, maximum security.

WILSON Yes, sir. Maximum security.

FRAZER *comes out of the office with the Lewis gun.*

JONES *(seeing the Lewis gun and reacting excitedly)* Whoop!

FRAZER Here you are, sir. It's all loaded and ready.

MAINWARING Right, set it up.

FRAZER *crosses to the stage, puts the Lewis gun on a card table and sits behind it.*

JONES Permission to speak, sir. How about cutting their trouser buttons off?

MAINWARING What?

During this speech, the CAPTAIN *moves up quietly behind* JONES.

JONES Well, sir, if we cut their trouser buttons off, and they try to run away, it will show at once that they are something unusual. Then a person walking along the street, nonchalant like, will see these men running, with their trousers round their ankles, and they will investigate.

CAPTAIN You!

JONES What?

CAPTAIN You don't dare do anything of the sort. The Geneva Convention clearly states that prisoners of war will not be put in humiliating positions.

JONES *gestures with his bayonet.*

JONES You'll be in a humiliating position, mate, if you get this up you.

CAPTAIN Don't threaten me, you silly old fool. *(He lights a cigarette)*

JONES You!!! You!!! *(He gestures at the* CAPTAIN *with his rifle)*

MAINWARING Jones. Jones! That will do, Jones.

JONES He called me a silly old fool, sir!

MAINWARING We're not savages. *(To the* CAPTAIN*)* You get back in your place and speak when you're spoken to.

WALKER Yeah that's right, get back in the huddle.

PIKE *comes out of the office with the Tommy gun.*

CAPTAIN I'm warning you, Captain.

MAINWARING *(in the* CAPTAIN*'s face)* Just do as you're told.

The CAPTAIN *blows smoke in* MAINWARING*'s face. He holds his expression for a while, but stifles a cough as he crosses to* WILSON.

You see the sort of *(he coughs)* insolent swine *(he coughs)* we're up against, Wilson?

WILSON Yes, sir. He has got rather an abrupt manner. But you must make allowances for him, he's probably upset because we sunk his submarine.

SPONGE *and* HANCOCK *enter with a stepladder.*

SPONGE Where do you want this stepladder, Mr Mainwaring?

MAINWARING Set it up here.

PIKE Here, Mr Sponge, I'll give you a hand.

MAINWARING Pike, get up there with your Tommy gun, then you've got a clear view of the entire hall.

PIKE You know I don't like going up ladders, Mr Mainwaring, with my vertigo.

MAINWARING Get up there at once, boy!

PIKE *starts to go up the ladder.*

PIKE It's ever so wobbly.

MAINWARING Get up!

PIKE I've got a note from the doctor.

MAINWARING Will you get up there! Godfrey—where's Godfrey?

GODFREY *is now dozing in a chair by the stage.*

Godfrey!

GODFREY *wakes with a start.*

GODFREY   Did you call, sir? *(He goes to* MAINWARING *slowly)* I'm terribly sorry, sir, I must have dozed off.

MAINWARING   Dozed off! Here we are guarding a dangerous gang of cutthroats and you doze off. You're supposed to watch him like a hawk, like a hawk. *(Pause)* Hold the ladder.

GODFREY   Yes, sir.

SPONGE *gets him a chair and he sits to hold the ladder. The phone rings.*

MAINWARING   Take charge, Wilson.

The lights fade down in the hall and the cast freeze. The lights fade up in the office.

MAINWARING *goes into the office, crosses to the desk and picks up the phone.*

Mainwaring here!

A spot comes up on the COLONEL *at his desk on the other side of the stage.*

COLONEL   GHQ here. Everything all right, Mainwaring?

MAINWARING   Yes, sir. I've got the prisoners safe and sound. They're all ready for you to pick up.

COLONEL   I'm afraid the escort won't be able to get over there until tomorrow morning.

MAINWARING   Do you mean to say that we've got to look after them all night?

COLONEL   Sorry, can't do anything about it. Just give them a blanket each and bed them down. And give them something to eat, of course.

MAINWARING   I'm afraid we've only got our own sandwiches, Colonel.

COLONEL Well, send out for some fish and chips.

MAINWARING Fish and chips!

COLONEL I'll see that you get the money back. Be over about eight in the morning. Cheerio.

MAINWARING *hangs up.*

The spot goes out on the COLONEL *and he exits.*

MAINWARING Fish and chips!

The lights crossfade from the office to the church hall.

(he quickly strides to the office door) Wilson!

WILSON Yes, sir. *(He joins* MAINWARING*)*

MAINWARING Come here—Jones! *(He gestures for him to join them)* The armed escort can't get over until the morning. They've got to be here all night.

JONES Well in that case, I really think we ought to cut their trouser buttons off, sir. *(He gestures with his bayonet)* Let me do it! Let me do it, sir!

MAINWARING Put that away, Jones. I shall have a word with the prisoners, Wilson.

WILSON You can't speak German, can you, sir...?

MAINWARING Oh, they'll know by the tone of my voice who's in charge. Believe me, Wilson, they recognize authority when they see it.

WILSON Yes, but—

MAINWARING *(concerned)* You'd better come with me.

WILSON Yes, sir.

They cross to the prisoners, followed by JONES.

MAINWARING Right now, pay attention.

The prisoners all come smartly to attention.

WILSON I say, they're awfully well disciplined, aren't they, sir?

MAINWARING Nothing of the sort. It's a slavish blind obedience. Not like the cheerful, light-hearted discipline that you get with our Jolly Jack Tars. I tell you they're a nation of unthinking automatons, led by a lunatic who looks like Charlie Chaplin.

CAPTAIN How dare you compare our glorious leader with that non-Aryan clown!

MAINWARING Now look here.

CAPTAIN *(taking out a notebook and pencil)* I am making a note of your insults, Captain, and your name will go on the list. And when we win the war, you will be brought to account.

MAINWARING You can write down what you like. You're not going to win this war.

CAPTAIN Oh yes we are.

MAINWARING Oh no you're not.

CAPTAIN Oh yes we are.

PIKE *(singing)*
"WHISTLE WHILE YOU WORK, HITLER IS A TWERP, HE'S HALF BARMY, SO'S HIS ARMY..."

The **CAPTAIN** *crosses to the ladder. The words die on* **PIKE**'s *lips.*

"Whistle..."

CAPTAIN Your name will also go on the list. What is it?

MAINWARING Don't tell him, Pike.

CAPTAIN Pike. Thank you.

MAINWARING *(boiling)* Now look here. I've had just about enough. Tell your men from me that they're going to be here all night and they'd better behave themselves. Now get on with it.

The CAPTAIN *shrugs his shoulders. During the following, he speaks to the prisoners in German.*

PIKE *(to* WILSON*)* Uncle Arthur.

WILSON Yes, what is it, Frank?

PIKE It's not fair that my name should be on the list. I was only joking.

WILSON You really should try and be more careful, Frank. You must realize by now that the Germans have absolutely no sense of humour.

PIKE But you've said much worse things about Hitler. *(Raising voice towards the* CAPTAIN*)* He's said much worse things.

WILSON Quiet, Frank. He'll hear you.

PIKE Do you think if you had a nice word with him, he'd take my name off the list?

WILSON OK I'll have a nice word.

MAINWARING *(to the* CAPTAIN*)* Have you told them what I said?

CAPTAIN Yes

MAINWARING Walker!

WALKER Yes, Captain Mainwaring.

They look around to check no-one is listening.

MAINWARING Is the fish and chip shop still open?

WALKER Yeh! I think so. Why?

MAINWARING *hands him a ten-shilling note.*

MAINWARING Here's ten shillings. Buy some for the prisoners. Jones. Wilson, a conference. *(He walks over to* WILSON *and* JONES*)*

WALKER *(taking out a notebook and licking a pencil)* Right then. One, two, three, four, five, six, seven, eight cod and chips.

CAPTAIN I want plaice.

WALKER Right. One plaice and chips and seven cod and chips. Right! Who wants vinegar?

CAPTAIN Wer mochte Essig? [*Who wants vinegar?*]

Four hold up their hands.

WALKER One, two, three, four, vinegar. Right. Who wants salt?

CAPTAIN Wer mochte Salz? [*Who wants salt?*]

Three hold up hands.

WALKER One, two, three for salt. Who doesn't want salt or vinegar?

CAPTAIN Wie viele ohne Salz und Essig? [*How many without salt and vinegar?*]

Two hands.

WALKER That's two without salt or vinegar. *(To the* CAPTAIN*)* 'Ere, c'mon now, let's see if I've got this right. Now, you want plaice and chips, and they're gonna have cod and chips. That's four with vinegar, three with salt and two without salt or vinegar.

MAINWARING *(approaching)* Walker! Walker! What do you think you're doing?

WALKER I'm taking the order.

CAPTAIN And I don't want nasty, soggy chips. I want mine crisp unt light brown.

WALKER *(writing it down)* Crisp unt light brown.

MAINWARING Never mind that rubbish! Now listen to me, if I say you'll eat soggy chips, you'll eat soggy chips.

The CAPTAIN *writes it on his notepad.*

WALKER *(also writing it down)* Soggy chips.

The tabs close and the lights fade to blackout. Music fades up as required to cover movement on stage.

Scene Four

The Church Hall. Later that night.

The tabs open, the music fades and the lights come up to full.

JONES is sitting behind the Lewis gun on the stage. WALKER and FRAZER are sitting beside him. WILSON is sitting in front of the stage, reading Picture Post. PIKE is up the ladder with the Tommy gun. GODFREY is sitting on a chair holding the ladder. MAINWARING is walking up and down, watching the prisoners, who are sitting on benches in the middle of the hall. The rest of the platoon are sitting in a circle round the prisoners. The CAPTAIN is smoking and following MAINWARING with his eyes all the time.

FRAZER Fancy giving those Germans fish and chips. All I've had to eat tonight is paste sandwiches.

JONES You've got to treat prisoners of war properly, you know, Jock. I shall never forget when we was in the Sudan, we had a young officer, Captain D'Arcy Holdane his name was, and he used to say, "Boys, always treat them Dervish prisoners well. See that they get plenty of betel-nut. If we treat them well, they'll learn by our example and treat us well." Anyhow, a few days later he was captured.

WALKER What happened to him?

JONES They chopped his head off.

FRAZER Look at the time. One o' clock in the morning. You'd think he'd let some of us take it in turns to sleep.

WALKER It's no use, Taff. Captain Mainwaring won't let us take our eyes off them. He's obsessed.

MAINWARING is still walking up and down. GODFREY stops him as he passes.

GODFREY Do you think I could possibly be excused, sir?

MAINWARING Certainly not. Stick to your post.

PIKE Yes, you hang on to this ladder, Mr Godfrey.

> **MAINWARING** *walks back towards the stage. He stops when he gets level with the* **CAPTAIN,** *who is watching him like a hawk. He moves and turns again, and waves his hand at the* **CAPTAIN.**

MAINWARING Don't keep staring at me all the time. Can't you look in another direction?

> *He walks towards the stage and as he passes* **WILSON** *he knocks his newspaper.*

Put that down, Wilson. I told you to watch the prisoners. *(He goes up on the stage)* Keep them well covered, Jones.

JONES Don't you worry, sir, I'm watching 'em.

FRAZER Yon captain never takes his eyes off you for a minute, Mr Mainwaring. If you were to ask my opinion, I don't think he likes you very much.

WALKER I wouldn't want to be in your shoes, sir, if he were to turn the tables on us.

MAINWARING There's not much chance of that, Walker.

> *The cast freeze as the lights crossfade to the office.*

> **HODGES** *and the* **VERGER** *enter the church hall office by the back door.*

HODGES Well I've had a good night tonight. I've booked three houses for showing lights and we've shared a bottle together, Mr Yeatman.

VERGER By the way, Mr Hodges, not a word to his reverence that I keep a bottle in my hidey hole.

HODGES You can rely on me. I'm the soul of discretion. Mum's the word. Better go and say good-night to Napoleon.

The lights crossfade to the hall.

HODGES *and the* **VERGER** *enter the hall.*

Good-night, Napoleon. *(He sees the prisoners)* Blimey, what's all this?

MAINWARING They're Nazi prisoners of war. Keep away from them.

VERGER You've no right to keep Germans in the church hall. The vicar will be furious.

MAINWARING You mind your own business.

The **CAPTAIN** *suddenly clutches his stomach and groans.*

HODGES What's the matter with you, mate?

CAPTAIN I feel so ill. *(He groans and slips to the floor)* It's my stomach.

HODGES 'Ere give me a hand, Verger.

They both cross to the **CAPTAIN.**

MAINWARING Get away from him.

HODGES What are you talking about? Can't you see the man's sick?

The **CAPTAIN** *is groaning and rolling on the floor.*

FRAZER He looks bad to me, sir.

WALKER Perhaps it was them soggy chips you made him eat.

MAINWARING *crosses to* **WILSON.**

WILSON I really think we ought to do something, sir.

MAINWARING I don't trust him, Wilson.

WILSON We can't just leave him lying there.

HODGES Well, don't stand there, Mainwaring. Do something. He's somebody's son, you know.

VERGER He's got a heart of stone, you know, Mr Hodges.

GODFREY There's some bicarbonate of soda in my first-aid kit if you think that will help.

MAINWARING Stay where you are, Godfrey.

PIKE Yes, don't let go of the ladder, Mr Godfrey.

MAINWARING Jones, keep them well covered. Watch them like a hawk, like a hawk do you understand?

JONES Yes, sir, I'm completely cocked.

MAINWARING And you, Pike, I'm going in.

> **FRAZER** *and* **WALKER** *come down from the stage with their rifles and bayonets.* **MAINWARING** *crosses to the* **CAPTAIN,** *who is cradled in* **HODGE***'s arms. The* **CAPTAIN** *gives another groan and passes out.*

There's something funny here.

HODGES What are you afraid of? They're only a few harmless German sailors.

> **MAINWARING** *kneels over the* **CAPTAIN.**

MAINWARING He seems to be breathing all right. How's his pulse?

> *Suddenly the* **CAPTAIN** *grabs* **MAINWARING***'s revolver, gets his arm round* **HODGE***'s neck and presses the revolver against it.*

CAPTAIN No-one is moving!

MAINWARING You, you...

CAPTAIN Hold as Maschienengewhr! [*Get the machine gun!*]

> *Two* **SAILORS** *advance on* **JONES,** *who picks up the Lewis gun and backs away.*

JONES Get back—you're not having it. Get back! Get back!

WILSON Please be careful, Jonesey.

The two **SAILORS** *jump up on the stage.* **JONES** *backs away, trips, the Lewis gun goes off and blows holes up the back wall and in the roof.* **PIKE** *falls off the ladder. Everyone dives for the floor as clouds of dust and bits of roof fall down.*

Blackout.

Scene Five

The Church Hall. Later that night.

The lights come up full on the office and the church hall.

MAINWARING *and the platoon are standing in a tight group in the middle of the hall, facing the door of the office.* **JONES** *is squatting behind the Lewis gun, which is on the card table.* **FRAZER, WALKER** *and* **PIKE** *are standing beside him with rifles and bayonets. The rest of the platoon are grouped round them, except* **SPONGE,** *Desmond and* **HANCOCK** *who are off stage. They all have fixed bayonets.* **GODFREY** *is hovering in the background.* **MAINWARING** *is in the middle with the Tommy gun. All weapons are pointed at the office door. In the office,* **HODGES** *is sitting at the desk. The* **CAPTAIN** *is standing beside him with the revolver stuck in* **HODGES'** *head. The rest of the* **SAILORS** *are standing round the desk, the* **VERGER** *is towards the back, standing nervously.*

WILSON *enters the church hall from the main doors.*

MAINWARING Everything all right, Wilson?

WILSON Yes, sir. I've posted Sponge, Hancock and Desmond outside. They've got the back door and window of the office covered.

MAINWARING That stupid drunken fool Hodges!

JONES I didn't let them have the gun, did I, sir?

MAINWARING No, you behaved very well, Jones.

JONES I haven't felt like that since I was in the trenches in 1916... I did do well, didn't I, Mr Wilson? Didn't I do well?

WILSON Yes you did, Jonesey, awfully well, very well indeed!

JONES Yes and you behaved well as well. You kept cool you did, you kept cool.

WILSON Oh you thought so did you, very cool was I?

FRAZER Hey hey hey, when you've quite finished this mutual admiration society, perhaps you'd like to tell us what we're going to do now, Captain Mainwaring?

WALKER He's right, we can't hang around here all night.

MAINWARING They've only got one revolver, and they can't get out of the office. Believe me, Walker, we hold all the trump cards.

The office door opens a few inches. They all cock their rifles. The VERGER's *hand comes round the door and waves a white handkerchief.*

MAINWARING Do they want to surrender, Verger?

VERGER No. I've got a message from the captain. He says he wants you to take him and his men back to the fishing boat so that they can cross to France.

MAINWARING He wants what!

VERGER If you don't agree to his terms, he's going to blow Mr Hodges' head off.

JONES Mr Mainwaring, if you let them escape back to France they'll get another submarine and start sinking British ships again.

WILSON Jones is right, I'm afraid, sir.

WALKER It's one man's life against thousands.

FRAZER A terrible decision you've got to make, Captain Mainwaring... But you must admit, you've never liked the man!

MAINWARING Tell him we need time to think it over.

VERGER Right.

He hurries back to the office. Inside the office HODGES *is still sitting at the desk with the* CAPTAIN *beside him with the revolver stuck in* **HODGES**' *neck. The rest of the* **SAILORS** *are standing round. The* **VERGER** *goes into the office.*

The lights fade down in the church hall and the cast freezes.

Scene Six

In the Office. Immediately following.

The lights fade up in the office.

CAPTAIN Well?

VERGER He's thinking it over.

CAPTAIN I'll give him until dawn.

HODGES What did Mainwaring say?

VERGER I must admit, Mr Hodges, it doesn't look good for you.

HODGES Oh no!

The lights fade in the office.

Scene Seven

In the Church Hall. Immediately following.

The lights come up in the church hall.

WALKER If only we could get that gun away from him somehow.

JONES Permission to speak, sir. I have an idea. Supposing I was to put on some old clothes, black my face, knock on the door and say I am a chimney sweep? And when I see Mr Hodges, I will say, "Hallo, Fritz". And they will say, "Why do you call him Fritz?" And I will say, "Because he is not British, he is a German prisoner of war, who works as an ARP Warden in his spare time".

MAINWARING Please, Jones.

JONES But it will sow the seeds of doubt in their minds, sir. And while the seeds are being sown, I will jump on the captain, and if the gun goes off, it might not hit Mr Hodges.

MAINWARING *gives* **JONES** *a look of despair.*

PIKE Mr Mainwaring, I saw a film called *The Petrified Forest.* And Humphrey Bogart was holding Leslie Howard by gunpoint in a cabin all night. And Leslie Howard kept quoting poetry and using long words. And it didn't half upset Humphrey Bogart. Perhaps you could do that.

WILSON I missed that film. What happened to Leslie Howard in the end?

PIKE He got shot.

MAINWARING You stupid boy.

GODFREY I saw Freddie Bartholomew in *David Copperfield,* sir. But there wasn't really anything in that.

MAINWARING I haven't heard so much drivel in all my life! ...*David Copperfield*! ...Wait a minute. Mr Micawber! "Something's bound to turn up." That's it. We'll play along with them. We've got to go through the town to get to the harbour. Someone's bound to raise the alarm. *(Shouting at the office)* All right, we agree to your terms. *(To* WILSON*)* Even if they get to the boat, Wilson, the Navy will blow them out of the water before they've gone a mile.

The office door opens and the CAPTAIN, *with* HODGES *at gunpoint, comes out of the office. The* VERGER *and the rest of the* SAILORS *follow.*

CAPTAIN I'm glad you have come to your senses, Captain. *(To one of the* SAILORS*)* Hold as Maschienengewhr! [*Get the machine gun!*] Passt auf die auf! [*Cover them!*] *(To the platoon)* Put down your rifles.

They hesitate.

MAINWARING Do as he says.

They pile their rifles on the floor.

CAPTAIN Get me a grenade and a piece of string.

MAINWARING See to that, Wilson.

WILSON Yes, sir. *(He goes into the office)*

CAPTAIN *(to the* SAILORS *in German)* Gewhre abladen und Bayonette abnehme. [*Unload the rifles, take the bayonets off.*]

They unload the rifles.

MAINWARING You won't get away with this. We're bound to be spotted going through the town.

CAPTAIN No-one will interfere, Captain, because you will be escorting us through the streets with empty rifles.

MAINWARING And how do you propose you're going to make us do that?

WILSON *returns with a Mills bomb and a piece of string.*

CAPTAIN Very simply.

He hands the revolver to one of the SAILORS, *who holds it against* HODGES's *neck. He takes the bomb and string from* WILSON.

Is it primed?

WILSON Oh yes.

The CAPTAIN *unscrews the base plug.*

CAPTAIN You don't mind if I make sure?

WILSON By all means.

The CAPTAIN *looks in the bomb.*

CAPTAIN Good. (*He screws back the base. To* JONES) You, old man, take off your belt and undo the back of your tunic.

JONES I beg your pardon?

CAPTAIN Do as I say. Remove your belt. (*He ties the end of the string to the ring of the pin*)

JONES *takes off his belt and unbuttons the back of his blouse.*

And just to make sure, Captain, that your behaviour is correct, the old man will march in front of me... (*He puts the bomb in the waistband of* JONES's *trousers. Pause*) One false move from you— (*Pause*) —and I pull the string. (*He buttons up the back of* JONES's *blouse*)

JONES Don't make any false moves, Mr Mainwaring, and don't make any real ones either!

CAPTAIN Seven seconds will give me plenty of time to get clear, but I think it is not enough time for the old man to unbutton his tunic.

FRAZER A terrible way to die.

MAINWARING You unspeakable swine. Now look here. I'm the commanding officer of this unit and as such I reserve the right to have the bomb in my waistband.

JONES I will not allow you to have a bomb in your trousers, sir. Don't you worry about me, they can put twenty bombs in my trousers and they will not make me crack.

MAINWARING You can't win this war! You see the sort of men this country breeds?

CAPTAIN Rather stupid ones.

MAINWARING You can sneer, but you've forgotten one thing, Captain.

CAPTAIN Oh yes, what is that?

MAINWARING The Royal Navy! You've got to cross twenty-five miles of water. You'll never make it.

CAPTAIN Oh yes we will, because all of you will be on the boat with us. *(Pointing to* **GODFREY***)* We shall leave the old man behind, to tell them. Your Navy won't fire on their own people. *(He takes* **MAINWARING***'s revolver, empties it and puts it back in the holster)* And when we get to France— *(Pause)* —you will be my prisoners— *(Pause)* —and then — *(Pause)* —we shall examine the list.

Blackout.

Scene Eight

In the street, on the way to the Harbour.

The half tabs are closed to hide the church hall. The lights fade up to full.

We see the procession marching along (on the spot for the purposes of dialogue once centre). MAINWARING *is in front and* HODGES *and the* VERGER *are marching level with him, the* CAPTAIN *is close behind him with the rest of the* SAILORS. *They are surrounded by* FRAZER, JONES, WALKER *and* GODFREY *and the rest of the platoon carrying rifles.* WILSON *and* PIKE *are in the rear.*

PIKE Uncle Arthur?

WILSON Yes!

PIKE If I tell the German there's a dummy detonator in the grenade, do you think he'll take my name off his list?

WILSON Be quiet, Frank!

The COLONEL *comes round the corner.*

WALKER Blimey, sir! Look, it's the colonel.

MAINWARING *(over his shoulder to the* CAPTAIN*)* The game's up! What are you going to do now?

CAPTAIN I am not going to do anything. You will bluff your way out.

MAINWARING I refuse to co-operate with you in any way whatsoever. He won't go through with it, Jones!

JONES Please, Mr Mainwaring, if you don't do as he says he'll pull the string.

MAINWARING Oh no he won't.

CAPTAIN Oh yes I will.

JONES He says he will, Mr Mainwaring.

They draw level with the **COLONEL**.

MAINWARING Platoon, halt!

COLONEL Where on earth are you taking the prisoners, Mainwaring?

MAINWARING The fact is sir, I—

WALKER We're going for a walk, sir. Captain Mainwaring thought it would be a good idea if we gave them a breath of fresh air. They've been cooped up in a submarine for weeks.

COLONEL What on earth's the matter with you, Mainwaring? You're as white as a sheet. You look as if you've seen a ghost.

FRAZER A breath of fresh air will do him the power of good, sir.

GODFREY We're taking them down to the harbour. The Sailors like a sea breeze.

COLONEL Well, all right then. I'm on my way to the railway station to pick up the escort for the prisoners. I'll see you later.

MAINWARING Yes sir, yes sir. Platoon, by the right, quick march!

They start to move.

COLONEL Wait a minute! Halt!

They halt.

You know, I'm surprised at you, Mainwaring. Your men are usually so smartly turned out. Why isn't Jones wearing his equipment? And what's that great lump of string hanging down his back?

MAINWARING Where?

COLONEL Here.

He pulls the string and holds it up. We see the pin on the end of it.

MAINWARING Oh no!

Everyone except the **COLONEL, JONES, WILSON, PIKE, MAINWARING, WALKER** *and* **FRAZER** *dive for cover and flatten themselves against the ground.* **MAINWARING, WALKER** *and* **PIKE** *try to get the bomb from* **JONES's** *trousers.*

JONES I've got a bomb in my trousers. Don't panic! Don't panic!

MAINWARING Get it out, Jones.

He starts to unbutton the back of his blouse. **HODGES** *is holding the* **VERGER,** *who has his fingers in his ears. The* **COLONEL** *looks on aghast.*

FRAZER I'll get it, sir, I'll get it.

JONES It's slipped down, sir. Save yourself, Mr Mainwaring.

WALKER Hang on, I'll cut it out. *(He goes at* **JONES** *with a bayonet)*

FRAZER *thrusts his arm down the back of* **JONES** *trousers.* **WILSON** *crosses to the* **COLONEL.**

WILSON I wonder if I might borrow your revolver, sir.

MAINWARING *and* **JONES** *are dancing in the road.*

JONES Don't panic, sir. Don't panic, sir.

COLONEL What the hell's going on?

WILSON I'll explain later. *(He waves the revolver at the prisoners)* Now listen to me, you German chaps. Would you mind awfully getting up against the wall, with your hands up please.

The prisoners obey.

Go on, do as you're told, there's good fellows.

MAINWARING Jones! Jones! Wait a minute. Wait a minute. It should have gone off by now.

They both stop.

JONES So it should. I've been saved, sir. I've been saved.

MAINWARING *crosses to* **WILSON**.

MAINWARING I thought I told you to prime those grenades.

WILSON I did, sir, with dummies.

MAINWARING Why is it you can never do anything you're... You've saved Jones's life, Wilson.

WILSON Well now perhaps you'll agree with me that it's awfully dangerous to keep them primed.

JONES Now that the crisis is past, Mr Mainwaring, would you mind asking Private Frazer to take his hand out of my trousers?

Blackout.

MUM'S ARMY

MUM'S ARMY

Original television transmission by the BBC on 20th November, 1970 with the following cast of characters:

CAPTAIN MAINWARING	Arthur Lowe
SERGEANT WILSON	John Le Mesurier
LANCE CORPORAL JONES	Clive Dunn
PRIVATE FRAZER	John Laurie
PRIVATE WALKER	James Beck
PRIVATE GODFREY	Arnold Ridley
PRIVATE PIKE	Ian Lavender
MRS GRAY	Carmen Silvera
EDITH PARISH	Wendy Richard
MRS PIKE	Janet Davies
MRS FOX	Pamela Cundell
MISS IRONSIDE	Julia Burbury
IVY SAMWAYS	Rosemary Faith
WAITRESS	Melita Manger
BUFFET ATTENDANT	Deirdre Costello
SERVICEMAN	David Gilchrist
MRS PROSSER	Eleanor Smale
PORTER	Jack Le White
PLATOON	Colin Bean, Hugh Hastings, Vic Taylor, Hugh Cecil, Desmond Cullum-Jones, Leslie Noyes, Freddie Wiles, George Hancock, Frank Godfrey, Freddie White
SERVICEMEN	Eric Stark, Les Conrad, David Melbourne, Peter Wilson
SERVICE GIRLS	Hilary Martin, Ann Downs, Carol Brett
CUSTOMERS	Clifford Hemsley, Maria Cope

CHARACTERS

CAPTAIN MAINWARING
SERGEANT WILSON
CORPORAL JONES
PRIVATE FRAZER
PRIVATE GODFREY
PRIVATE WALKER
PRIVATE PIKE
PRIVATE SPONGE
PRIVATE HANCOCK
MRS FOX
IVY SAMWAYS
EDITH PARISH
MRS GRAY
MISS IRONSIDE
MRS PIKE
WAITRESS
MRS PROSSER
SERVICEMAN
OTHER MEMBERS OF THE PLATOON
RAIL PASSENGERS

The action takes place in Walmington-on-Sea on the south coast of England

Time—1940

Scene One

The Church Hall. Night.

The platoon is on parade. **MAINWARING** *and* **WILSON** *are in their usual positions.* **JONES** *is at the far end, away from them.*

MAINWARING Platoon—stand at ease.

JONES is late.

Platoon—'shun!

JONES is late.

WILSON Try to do it with the others, Jones.

JONES Sorry, sir.

MAINWARING Thank you, Wilson. Platoon—stand at ease.

JONES is late yet again.

JONES I think what is causing it, sir, is that—you being at the end of the line—the sound of your command is taking longer to cross the air to reach me, sir.

MAINWARING Yes—it must be something like that.

WALKER Perhaps, if you was to nod your head, sir, he would catch on a bit quicker.

JONES That's right, sir, you nod yer head, sir, and I'll not be found wanting.

MAINWARING I don't think we'll get involved with that, Jones. Now, pay attention. Some of your uniforms are looking pretty shoddy and one or two badges could do with brassing up a bit. Now, this brings me to a little scheme that we have been discussing—haven't we, Wilson?

WILSON That's right, sir.

MAINWARING *nods.*

JONES *(coming suddenly to attention)* H'up.

MAINWARING What's the matter, Jones?

JONES You nodded, sir, so I sprung to it.

MAINWARING We're not doing that, Jones.

JONES I'm sorry, sir.

MAINWARING Now, we've been approached by several of the womenfolk.

JONES Ay 'up. *(He stands at ease)*

MAINWARING What's the matter now, Jones?

JONES I was standing at attention, sir. Now I'm easing myself.

MAINWARING We have been approached by several of the womenfolk, who would like to join with us in our fight against the common foe. Wilson and I think this is quite a good scheme—don't we, Wilson?

WILSON Yes, sir. Don't nod, will you, sir?

MAINWARING I'll watch it. They could take over some of the paperwork and the making of tea and cocoa, etc...

FRAZER Buttons!

MAINWARING I beg your pardon, Frazer?

FRAZER Buttons, sir. They could sew on buttons.

MAINWARING Precisely—a very good point. Make a note of that, Wilson.

WILSON Yes, sir.

MAINWARING *(nodding)* A very good point, indeed.

JONES *(jumping to attention)* Ay 'up.

MAINWARING Jones!

JONES You nodded, sir. Oh—sorry, sir—I forgot we wasn't doing it.

MAINWARING *(to* **WILSON***)* We're going to have to let him go.

GODFREY My sister is very good at sewing—petit point and all that sort of thing—providing someone else will thread the needle.

MAINWARING I think perhaps we should concentrate on rather a younger age group, Godfrey.

PIKE There's a new girl at the sweet shop—she's very obliging.

MAINWARING That sounds more like the girl we need.

WALKER That's right—comforts for the troops.

MAINWARING We don't want any of that sort of talk, Walker.

FRAZER There's a lassie works for the Gaslight and Coke Company. She's a good weight-bearing sonsie girl with a firm body and big strong thighs.

JONES They're very strong—the ones with big thighs.

MAINWARING Well, I'm sure between us, we can round up the right sort of material. What does sonsie mean?

WILSON An obscure Scottish term.

MAINWARING Anyway, bring them along to the office tomorrow. We only need a handful. Properly trained, they'll release us—the frontline troops—so that we can grapple with the enemy.

WALKER I don't suppose Taffy and Jones' ere will have much energy left after grappling with those big thighs.

MAINWARING Walker, I shan't tell you again.

Blackout.

Scene Two

In the Office and the Church Hall. Night.

WILSON *is in the office at the desk doing some work. In the church hall stands a group:* **JONES** *is waiting with* **MRS FOX;** **PIKE** *is with* **IVY SAMWAYS**—*a very quiet, retiring girl;* **FRAZER** *is without his girl;* **WALKER** *has brought* **EDITH PARISH** *who is a blonde, forthcoming cockney.*

MAINWARING *enters the office by the outside door.*

MAINWARING Ah, good-evening, Wilson. How goes the recruiting?

WILSON The men seem to have brought quite a few along.

MAINWARING Right, we'd better bash on. Get them in—one at a time.

WILSON *crosses to the hall door.*

WILSON Ah, now, who's first?

JONES This is Mrs Fox, Sergeant.

WILSON Ah, yes, Mrs Fox. I wonder if you would be so kind as to come in.

MRS FOX Oo—thanks ever so.

MRS FOX *comes into the office with* **JONES.**

WILSON What an awfully humid day it's been.

MRS FOX Yes, hasn't it.

WILSON Still—you're looking marvellously cool. This is Mrs Fox, sir.

MAINWARING *(standing and saluting)* How do you do, Mrs Fox.

MRS FOX Nicely, thank you.

JONES She's one of my best customers, sir. I think you will find she will give every satisfaction.

MAINWARING Thank you, Jones.

WILSON By Jove, how rude of me—please have a chair. *(He draws up a chair)* Now, is there anything we can get you? Would you like a nice cup of tea or something?

MRS FOX Oh, I don't think so.

MAINWARING Wilson.

WILSON The kettle's on, it won't take a moment.

MRS FOX Well...

MAINWARING Wilson, I would like a word with you outside for a moment. Please excuse me, Mrs Fox.

He takes **WILSON** *into the church hall.*

Wilson, I know you are something of a ladies' man, but these women are going to be subject to discipline like the rest of our force. Let's start as we mean to go on, shall we?

WILSON Well, surely we can be polite!

MAINWARING I quite agree, but we don't have to have all this Jack Buchanan stuff. We'll just stick to the business in hand, if you don't mind.

WILSON Whatever you say, sir.

They return to the office.

MAINWARING Sorry about that, Mrs Fox. Name—Fox. Christian name?

MRS FOX Marcia.

MAINWARING *(writing)* Marcia.

WILSON What a pretty name,

MRS FOX Do you think so?

WILSON It's one of my favourites.

MAINWARING Wilson!

MRS FOX *(handing over a card)* Oh, there's my address. *(Confidentially)* I've written my age on the bottom.

MAINWARING Thank you.

MRS FOX *(turning to* **JONES***)* I was just telling Mr Mainwaring— I've written my age on the bottom.

> **JONES** *thinks this is a very strange thing to have done.*

MAINWARING Occupation?

MRS FOX Widow.

MAINWARING Is that an occupation?

WILSON *(being charming again)* In Mrs Fox's case, I would say it was almost a calling.

MAINWARING *(throwing down the pencil)* Wilson!

WILSON Sorry, sir.

JONES Mrs Fox is a very fine looking lady, sir—and a most understanding and warm female person.

MAINWARING Well, I'm sure that will be most useful. Would you like to join us?

MRS FOX I didn't know you'd come apart.

> **WILSON** *laughs cordially.* **MAINWARING** *is deadpanned.*

WILSON Awfully good—don't you think so, sir?

MAINWARING I'll take that as an affirmative answer. Thank you, Mrs Fox. Next one please, Wilson.

WILSON This way, Mrs Fox.

> **WILSON** *shows* **MRS FOX** *out to the hall.*

MRS FOX *(as she goes)* Thank you, Mr Mainwaring.

JONES (*leaning over the desk*) She's a very dry wit, sir, is Mrs Fox.

MAINWARING Yes, I'm sure. Thank you, Jones.

> WILSON *ushers* PIKE *and* IVY SAMWAYS *into the office.*

PIKE Oh, this is the young lady I was telling you about, sir. Ivy Samways.

MAINWARING Ivy Samways.

WILSON You may remember, sir—she was the one who was very obliging.

MAINWARING Thank you, Wilson.

> JONES *looks at* IVY.

There's no need for you to stay, Jones.

JONES Thank you, sir.

> JONES *starts to go back to the church hall with elaborate about turns, left turns, right turns, etc.*

MAINWARING Now, you're a shop assistant, aren't you?

> JONES *salutes.*

Get out, Jones.

> JONES *goes into the hall.*

You're a shop assistant, aren't you?

She nods.

Address?

IVY (*completely inaudible*) Twenty-seven, Jutland Drive.

MAINWARING I beg your pardon?

IVY (*inaudibly again*) Twenty-seven, Jutland Drive.

MAINWARING I... I'm afraid I didn't quite catch that.

PIKE Jutland Drive, sir.

MAINWARING Oh, Jutland Drive. *(He writes)* What number?

IVY *(inaudibly)* Twenty-seven.

MAINWARING Umh?

IVY *(inaudibly again)* Twenty-seven.

PIKE Twenty-seven...sir.

MAINWARING Ah...now I wonder what sort of task we can find to fit Miss Samways.

WILSON Answering the telephone, sir?

MAINWARING You're trying my patience rather far today, Wilson.

WILSON She can look after the secrets file, sir, most admirably.

MAINWARING Right...thank you, Miss Samways.

> FRAZER *pops into the office.* PIKE *and* IVY *go back to the hall. During the following,* WALKER *comes into the office with* EDITH PARISH.

FRAZER A word, sir?

MAINWARING Yes, Frazer.

FRAZER The lassie from the Gaslight and Coke Company cannot be here tonight, sir, but I have asked her, and she wants to join. She's just the sort we want, sir. A fine, firmly built girl—you know—strong...with big thighs.

MAINWARING Yes...thank you, Frazer. Bring her tomorrow.

> WALKER *is in front of the desk with* EDITH PARISH.

WALKER Er, Mr Mainwaring, this is Edith Parish—she's a friend of mine.

MAINWARING I see...do you have an occupation, Miss Parish?

EDITH Yeh—I'm an usherette.

WALKER That's right—the Tivoli Cinema—you know—with the torch.

MAINWARING Ah... I expect you see a lot of pictures.

EDITH Yeah... I see a lot of other things an' all.

WALKER *(confidentially)* Any time you want to see a film... knock three times on the fire exit round the side alley and she'll fit you in.

MAINWARING Y-e-s, well, I don't think I shall be taking advantage of your hospitality, Miss Parish. Now, where do you live?

EDITH Down Berwick Road—thirty-five—I live with my dad and he's six foot three—so you needn't get any ideas.

MAINWARING I think that will be all, Miss Parish.

WALKER I'll see that she's here tomorrow, sir.

> **WALKER** *and* **EDITH** *go back to the hall.*

(to EDITH, *as they go)* You shouldn't have said that to 'im— he don't get ideas.

> **WILSON** *and* **MAINWARING** *are alone in the office.*

MAINWARING I don't think that is the right class of girl for us at all, Wilson. Are there any more?

WILSON No, that's all, sir.

MAINWARING Send the men home then, Wilson. They were very late last night. I'll sort some of this out.

WILSON Very good, sir. *(He goes into the hall)* Er, right—that's all for tonight, ladies and gentlemen. I hope you've enjoyed it, and we'll look forward to seeing you at the same time tomorrow.

Everyone starts to exit.

The lights fade to blackout.

Off you go then.

Scene Three

In the Church Hall and Office. Immediately following.

There's a knock on the outside door.

MAINWARING Come in.

MRS GRAY *enters. She is a good-looking, middle-aged woman with great charm, very neatly dressed.*

MRS GRAY Captain Mainwaring?

MAINWARING That's right.

MRS GRAY I heard you were needing women helpers for the Home Guard—is that right?

MAINWARING Yes, yes, quite correct. Do sit down.

MRS GRAY I've heard about this platoon since its very beginning. I think you've done a wonderful job.

MAINWARING Well, we just try to do our best for old England in her hour of need.

MRS GRAY I'd love to help. Just to feel that I was doing something.

MAINWARING Your face seems vaguely familiar. Have I seen you at the Golf Club?

MRS GRAY No... I've not been in Walmington long. I had to bring my mother away from London because of the bombing.

MAINWARING I see.

MRS GRAY I'd loved to have stayed—not that there was much that I could have done, but just being there would have shown that wretched little Hitler that we're not going to give in.

MAINWARING By Jove—that's the sort of talk I like to hear. *(Getting down to business)* Now, what's the name?

MRS GRAY Gray.

MAINWARING And the Christian name?

MRS GRAY Fiona.

MAINWARING Fiona—what a pretty name.

MRS GRAY Do you think so?

MAINWARING It has always been one of my favourites.

MRS GRAY Thank you.

MAINWARING Occupation?

MRS GRAY Well...widow, I suppose—if you can call that an occupation.

MAINWARING Well, in your case I would say it was almost a... *(He decides not to say it, and instead writes)* Widow—and the address?

MRS GRAY Thirty-one, Wilton Gardens.

MAINWARING Wilton Gardens! That's quite near me.

MRS GRAY I know... I see you go to the bank every morning.

MAINWARING I say, do you really?

MRS GRAY And how marvellously punctual you are. We thought you were three minutes late the other day.

MAINWARING Was I?

MRS GRAY No. The clock was wrong.

MAINWARING Oh well...in my position one must set an example to the youngsters.

MRS GRAY Oh, I agree. All the old standards are declining so rapidly.

MAINWARING They are—indeed they are.

She looks at him. He looks at her.

MRS GRAY Well, I mustn't keep you.

MAINWARING Shall we see you tomorrow night, then? We usually parade about seven o'clock.

MRS GRAY I can't wait to start. At the moment my life consists of morning coffee at Ann's Pantry and making the dahlias grow.

MAINWARING I'm very fond of dahlias.

MRS GRAY Really? Do you grow them, too?

MAINWARING No—no, unfortunately. My wife says they attract earwigs.

MRS GRAY What a shame, but she's quite right. *(She gathers her bag and gloves)* Captain Mainwaring, may I say something awfully personal?

MAINWARING Well, of course.

MRS GRAY Do you always wear spectacles?

MAINWARING Well, yes I do.

MRS GRAY Would you take them off for a moment?

MAINWARING Well, er, yes, if you wish. *(He takes them off)*

MRS GRAY That's so much better—I always think they act as a sort of...well...they cut off the warmth in a person's eyes – just as a fireguard takes away so much of the heat.

MAINWARING Yes, I suppose you're right. I... I've never thought of it that way.

WILSON *enters from the hall door.*

MAINWARING *hastily replaces his glasses.*

WILSON Oh—still here, sir?

MAINWARING Ah...Sergeant Wilson—this is a new recruit – Mrs Fiona Gray.

WILSON Fiona! I say, what a pretty—

MAINWARING *(interrupting)* Yes...well... I have all the details, Mrs Gray, and I'll see you tomorrow at seven thirty.

MRS GRAY I shall look forward to it.

MRS GRAY *goes.*

MAINWARING Most charming woman that, Wilson.

WILSON Is she, sir?

MAINWARING Just the sort of material we need.

WILSON Well, you're such a good judge as a rule, it will be most interesting to see how they all shape up.

Blackout.

Scene Four

The Church Hall and the Office. The following night.

The girls and the platoon, including, **FRAZER**, **JONES**, **WALKER**, **PIKE** *and* **GODFREY**, *are in the hall.* **FRAZER**'s *girl,* **MISS IRONSIDE**, *is apart from the rest.* **FRAZER** *crosses to* **JONES**.

FRAZER There she is, Jones, over there.

JONES *looks.*

JONES I don't think she's got big thighs, Mr Frazer. Long ones maybe.

FRAZER What's the matter with your eyes, man. They're like tree trunks.

The lights come up on the office.

There are dahlias on **MAINWARING**'s *desk and the whole place is neater than usual.*

MAINWARING *enters from the outside door. He goes to the desk and puts down his stick and gloves. He sees the dahlias. He is pleased. He crosses to the mirror, he removes his glasses and admires the result with some difficulty. He puts them in his top pocket.*

WILSON *calls to* **MRS PIKE** *from outside.*

WILSON *(offstage)* Go through the main door, Mavis, and we'll be with you in a moment.

WILSON *enters the office from outside. During the following,* **MRS PIKE** *enters the hall from the main door.*

Ah, good-evening, sir.

MAINWARING Good-evening, Wilson.

WILSON Dear, dear, have you broken your glasses, sir?

MAINWARING No, Wilson, I just left them off for a moment. *(He puts them on again)* Right, let's get on with it.

MAINWARING *goes into the hall, followed by* WILSON.

WILSON Platoon—'shun!

WALKER, FRAZER, JONES, PIKE *and* GODFREY *are in the front row with their girls in the row behind them.*

MAINWARING Now, welcome, ladies.

LADIES Good-evening. *(Etc.)*

MAINWARING Since sooner or later we will be getting you uniforms, I thought it best today to teach you just the rudiments of foot drill, so that we can look like a disciplined body of men and—er women. Now, first of all—the "at ease" position. The legs should be comfortably apart—about eighteen inches or so.

They do so.

The hands are placed right over left—just over your bot... over your beh...at the back. Have you all got that?

MRS PIKE A lot of red tape nonsense.

PIKE No talking in the ranks, Mum.

MAINWARING Pike. No talking in the ranks. Now, to come to attention—you transfer your weight on to your right foot.

They lean.

You raise your left foot. I'm doing it in slow motion, of course, and—then place your left foot beside your right.

MAINWARING *totters and* WILSON *steadies him.*

Thus. Now, here's the tricky bit. At the same time, bring your hands to your sides, with thumbs in line with the seams of your trousers.

JONES Permission to speak, sir? These ladies are not wearing trousers, sir—them being ladies.

WALKER They can put their thumbs in line with the seams of their knickers.

MAINWARING Walker, fall out and stand over there. You will take no further part in this parade.

WALKER *(moving to the side)* Blimey, what have I said?

EDITH If we wasn't wearing 'em, he'd have something to go on about.

GODFREY *(to the ladies behind him)* He's very coarse, but very good-hearted.

MAINWARING Right, now, let's try it. Give the command, Wilson.

WILSON Squad—'shun.

They come to attention.

MAINWARING Oh, no—that was very sloppy. Not you, Mrs Gray, that was very good. You must all stand up straight. Stomachs in, chests out.

JONES Not you, Mrs Fox, that's very good.

MAINWARING Right, now, let's go once more. Stand at ease. Squad, 'shun...

They do so. **MRS FOX** *is behind the others.*

Now, come along, Mrs Fox.

JONES Yes, come along, you're all behind.

MRS FOX I was following you.

JONES You mustn't undermine my position, you know.

MAINWARING Stand at ease.

MRS PIKE Silly red tape.

PIKE Mum, no talking in the ranks.

MAINWARING Pike! I shan't tell you again.

FRAZER Captain Mainwaring. Miss Ironside here is doing it very well. Her legs are going with a very firm, strong action.

MAINWARING Yes, thank you, Frazer. *(To* WILSON*)* She doesn't seem to have very big thighs to me, Wilson.

WILSON Quite long, though.

MAINWARING Yes, now, let's move on to left and right turn. Now to turn right, you swivel on the right heel and left toe—thus. One—two, one—two.

> MAINWARING *demonstrates and totters a little.* WILSON *helps him.* WALKER *hums.*

Walker! Now brace the rear thigh hard as you go.

FRAZER Ay, that's right. Do as the captain says—those thighs have to be braced firm and strong.

MAINWARING Yes, thank you, Frazer. Then you lift the rear leg high, and place it beside the front one.

EDITH Blimey—what a way to win the war.

GODFREY You'll find the captain knows best, if you'd listen to him.

MAINWARING Godfrey, face front and don't keep staring at the ladies.

WALKER Woman mad—woman mad 'e is.

MAINWARING Any more from you and you'll be sent home.

> WALKER *reacts.*

Look to your front. Now, let's try it. Squad—'shun. Very good, Mrs Gray.

> MRS GRAY *reacts.*

Squad—left turn.

They turn different ways.

Ah—face your front.

WILSON There seems to be a little confusion as to which is which, sir.

MAINWARING I know, Wilson.

JONES They had the same trouble, sir, during the American Civil War, when they had to have all sorts of crude, rough, country yokel men as soldiers and they didn't know their left foot from their elbow, sir. So, to overcome this ingeniously, they tied a piece of hay to one foot and a piece of straw to the other, and when they wanted to turn left, the commanding man said "Hay turn" or "Straw turn"—according to whether the hay was on the left foot or the straw was on the left foot. Mind you, they had to be careful to get straws on all the left feet or hay, as the case may be. Do you think that would help, sir?

WALKER I think that's a good idea, sir. Then you would be able to come in and say, "Good-evening, ladies, what nice straws you are wearing."

MAINWARING That's it—go home, Walker.

WALKER I didn't say anything.

MAINWARING I'm not arguing—it's an order.

The lights fade to blackout.

Scene Five

Ann's Pantry. Day.

The café is two or three tables wide by two or three tables deep. There is a window and a door to the street.

GODFREY, *in his everyday clothes, is sitting by the window, concealed by a newspaper.*

MAINWARING *enters. He is in his business suit. He selects a table in the foreground, looks round and sits. He removes his spectacles, and takes up his paper. He can't see it, so he puts his specs on again.*

MRS GRAY *enters. She is about to sit at the next table when she sees* **MAINWARING.**

MRS GRAY Oh, good-morning, Mr Mainwaring.

MAINWARING *(rising)* Ah, what a surprise. Won't you join me?

MAINWARING *takes off his spectacles.* **GODFREY** *drops his newspaper. He reacts to the scene.*

MRS GRAY Thank you. *(She sits)* I haven't seen you here before.

MAINWARING Oh, I come here from time to time, you know— when I get my nose away from the grindstone.

The **WAITRESS** *brings the menu.*

WAITRESS Yes, please?

MAINWARING *(taking it)* Ah, thank you. *(He can't read it, so he puts on his spectacles and looks)* Ah, oh no, I don't think I'll bother with any of that. *(He realizes that* **MRS GRAY** *should have it first)* Oh, I do beg your pardon. *(He hands it to her and takes off his spectacles)*

MRS GRAY No, just coffee for me, as usual.

MAINWARING Yes, that's a capital idea—coffee, please.

The **WAITRESS** *goes.*

They used to do the most marvellous Devonshire teas here, you know.

MRS GRAY With jam and cream?

MAINWARING That's right.

The **WAITRESS** *enters and gives* **GODFREY** *his bill and then exits.*

I remember just after the last war. I'd just joined the Guildford branch—a chum and I borrowed a flivver and took a spin down here to Ann's Pantry, just for the Devonshire tea. When I got home, I had the rough end of my governor's tongue, I can tell you. He thought I had toddled off with a bit of fluff.

MRS GRAY Oh, it was all harmless fun, in those days.

MAINWARING Of course it was. Mind you, we used to go the pace now and then. *(He laughs reminiscently)*

MRS GRAY You know, your whole face seems to light up when you laugh. I think you're a very jolly person at heart.

MAINWARING Yes, I think I probably am. Mind you, bank managers don't get much chance of joking and jesting.

The **WAITRESS** *delivers the coffee.*

WAITRESS Separate bills?

MRS GRAY Yes, please.

MAINWARING No, no please. Have it with me.

GODFREY *passes by to pay the bill.*

GODFREY Good-morning, Captain Mainwaring.

MAINWARING Godfrey, is it?

GODFREY I haven't seen you in here before.

MAINWARING Oh, I pop in from time to time, you know.

GODFREY I'm just on my way to the clinic. *(He sees* **MAINWARING** *properly)* Oh, dear—have you broken your spectacles, Mr Mainwaring?

MAINWARING Oh, no—just giving my eyes a rest, you know.

GODFREY Well, will you excuse me?

GODFREY *pays the* **WAITRESS** *and goes.*

MAINWARING *(to* MRS GRAY*)* A charming man—one of my most loyal soldiers.

WALKER *enters. He is dressed in civilian clothes and has a small suitcase.*

MRS GRAY They're a wonderful band of men.

MAINWARING I'm very proud of them.

WALKER *comes to the table.*

WALKER 'Allo, Captain Mainwaring—haven't seen you here before.

MAINWARING Well, I come in from time to time.

WALKER 'Ere, if you've bust your specs, I know a bloke that's got five hundred frames—hardly used.

MAINWARING No, I haven't broken them, thank you.

WALKER 'Ere, if anyone asks you—you haven't seen me. I'm just delivering a bit of the sweet stuff—savvy?

MAINWARING You mean—sugar?

WALKER Shhh—you haven't seen me. *(He moves off and comes quickly back)* I haven't seen you too, so don't worry.

WALKER *goes.*

MRS GRAY *reacts.*

MAINWARING Heart of gold that man—do anything for you. What part of London do you come from?

MRS GRAY Oh, just near Regent's Park. Of course it was hopeless for Mother. They have the ack-ack guns there, you know. Oh dear, was that careless talk?

MAINWARING That's all right — any secret is quite safe with me.

JONES, *in his everyday clothes, enters with* MRS PROSSER.

JONES Hallo, Mr Mainwaring, don't often see you 'ere.

MAINWARING I do come in—

JONES This is Mrs Prosser. This is Mr Mainwaring.

MAINWARING How do you do. Er—this is Mrs Gray.

MRS GRAY How do you do.

JONES *(to* MRS PROSSER*)* You sit there, my dear. I'll join you in a moment. *(To* MAINWARING*)* Mrs Prosser is a very good friend of mine, sir, but there is nothing in it.

MAINWARING Oh, I see.

JONES All the same, you won't tell Mrs Fox you've seen me with her, will you, sir? It's just that I give her pieces for her cat and on 'er part she keeps me company from time to time.

MAINWARING Thank you, Jones.

JONES *sits at* MRS PROSSER's *table.*

I'm sorry about all these interruptions. I must say I was looking forward to a nice cup of coffee and a quiet chat.

MRS GRAY So was I.

MAINWARING I have to confess I came here quite deliberately on the chance you'd be here.

MRS GRAY I'd rather hoped you might.

PIKE *enters and comes to the table. He is wearing a suit.*

PIKE Captain Mainwaring, Mr Wilson says he is sorry to spoil your *tête-à- tête,* but the bank inspectors are here and will you come straight away.

MAINWARING Yes, right—all right, Pike—I'm coming. *(To* MRS GRAY*)* I'm sorry about this. Let's meet again very soon.

MRS GRAY I'd like that.

MAINWARING I shall see you tonight anyway, on parade.

MRS GRAY Yes, of course, I'll look forward to it.

MAINWARING So will I—sorry, I must go.

MAINWARING *exits.*

The WAITRESS *approaches.*

WAITRESS Two coffees—that's one and tuppence.

MRS GRAY *realizes he hasn't paid, smiles and reaches for her handbag.*

Blackout.

Scene Six

The Church Hall and the Office. Night.

JONES, FRAZER, PIKE, GODFREY, WALKER, *and all the ladies, with the exception of* **MRS GRAY,** *are talking amongst themselves in the hall.* **MAINWARING** *is at the desk in the office. The men are wearing their uniforms.*

FRAZER Yon Mainwaring's making an utter fool of himself. There's no other way of putting it.

EDITH Three times they come last week to see *Forty Little Mothers* with Eddie Cantor and they come again last night to see *Shipyard Sally* with Gracie Fields... Shirley shows them in, so they think I don't see, but they're always in the back row—only holding hands, mind. Not like some people I know who seem to have more arms than an octopus.

This last remark was for **WALKER***'s benefit but* **JONES** *takes it.*

JONES I've a very possessive nature, Miss Parish.

WILSON *enters, and hears some of the gossip.*

PIKE They have coffee every morning together.

GODFREY I've not seen them.

PIKE They go to the Dutch Oven now, I have to come and get 'im if there's anything important.

FRAZER Folly, sheer folly—it'll be the ruin of him—somebody should tell him.

GODFREY Well, I think it is none of our business. We shouldn't talk about that sort of thing behind their backs.

WALKER Blimey, you're one to talk. It was you what told us about them playing clock golf at the municipal gardens.

GODFREY I thought... I thought it was rather nice.

The lights come up on the office.

MAINWARING *is at his desk.*

WILSON *goes into the office.*

MAINWARING Ah, good-evening, Wilson. It's about time for parade, isn't it?

WILSON Just a few more minutes, I think, sir.

MAINWARING Good. I have rather an important announcement to make concerning the ladies' section.

WILSON Ah, yes—the ladies' section. Er—I did rather want to talk to you about that some time.

MAINWARING Oh, yes?

WILSON I know it is none of my business, but if I don't say something, well... I mean who will?

MAINWARING What are you talking about, Wilson?

WILSON Well, we've know each other a long time—in the bank, with the platoon. You might almost say we're practically friends—nearly?

MAINWARING Wilson—if you have something to say—stop shuffling from one foot to another and cough it up. Are you in some sort of trouble?

WILSON Good Lord, no. It's just that, with the ladies' section, do you think it is just possible that some of us are making tiny little fools of ourselves?

MAINWARING Ah... I see. Well, I appreciate your frankness, Wilson.

WILSON Thank you, sir.

MAINWARING It can't have been easy for you to talk to me on such a delicate matter.

WILSON Well, I only did it for the best, sir.

MAINWARING I'm not insensitive to what people have been saying, so I've decided to dismiss the female section and just hang on to one or two special helpers.

WILSON I see, sir.

MAINWARING So that should solve your problem and get Mrs Pike out of your hair. Come along, I'll make the announcement.

MAINWARING *goes into hall.* **WILSON** *follows.*

Right—pay attention please. Is everybody here, Jones?

JONES Everybody, except Mrs Gray, sir...that is.

MAINWARING Mrs Gray, not here? How strange—perhaps she is a little bit under the weather.

FRAZER Favouritism.

PIKE Ivy says she thinks she is all right, because she saw her carrying two big, heavy cases to the station.

MAINWARING The station!

IVY *whispers to* **PIKE.**

PIKE About ten minutes ago.

MAINWARING Ten minutes ago! You saw her go to the station.

WALKER There's only one train, the eight forty to London.

MAINWARING Take the parade, Wilson.

MAINWARING *hurries out through the office.*

WILSON *(calling after him)* Do you want me to make the announcement?

MAINWARING *has gone.*

Oh, Lord.

Blackout.

Scene Seven

The Station Waiting Room and Platform. A little later.

It is small and dimly lit by gas. There is one small refreshment counter with a hot-water machine, some tired-looking sandwich cases, etc. **MRS GRAY** *is at the counter getting a cup of tea.*

MRS GRAY Not too strong, thank you.

GIRL Not much chance of that, dear. Anything else?

MRS GRAY No, thank you.

GIRL Just tuppence then.

MRS GRAY *pays and takes the tea to a table.*

MAINWARING *enters. He sees her and crosses. During the following, a* **SERVICEMAN** *enters and goes to the counter to get a cup of tea.*

MAINWARING What's this then, what's happened?

MRS GRAY Nothing's happened, I'm just going back to London, that's all.

MAINWARING How long for?

MRS GRAY I don't know—a month or two—for good perhaps.

MAINWARING Why? You never mentioned it—you never even hinted.

MRS GRAY I just thought it would be best.

MAINWARING But I don't want you to go. My whole life is completely different. I just live from one meeting to the next.

MRS GRAY I know—I'm just the same, but it's the only thing to do. People are talking.

MAINWARING People always talk—who cares about that?

MRS GRAY But there's your wife.

MAINWARING They won't talk to her. She's not left home since Munich.

MRS GRAY Be sensible, George. You can't afford to have scandal and tittle tattle.

MAINWARING I don't care.

MRS GRAY But there's the bank.

MAINWARING Damn the bloody bank!

MRS GRAY George!

MAINWARING I'm sorry, but don't take that train.

MRS GRAY George, I must.

MAINWARING I implore you—don't take that train; we'll only see each other once a week.

MRS GRAY You're making this very difficult for me, but I've made up my mind—it's the only way.

The sound of a train approaching in the distance.

PORTER'S VOICE Victoria—Victoria train.

MRS GRAY There's my train.

MAINWARING Fiona. I've never begged anyone for anything in my life, but I'm begging you not to go. *(He rises)*

The SERVICEMAN *comes up with a cup of tea.*

SERVICEMAN Finished with those chairs, mate?

MAINWARING Yes, take the damn things.

SERVICEMAN Oh, all right, I only asked.

MRS GRAY I'm sorry, George. *(She picks up her cases and moves to the door)*

MAINWARING Here, that's heavy, let me.

He helps her with the case. They move on to the platform. **MAINWARING** *is separated from* **MRS GRAY** *a little.*

Look, let's talk about it. Go tomorrow.

The train stops. She struggles towards a compartment. He follows her.

PORTER'S VOICE Walmington-on-Sea. Walmington-on-Sea. Victoria train.

The lights fade.

Scene Eight

A Train Compartment. Immediately following.

There are seven people in the compartment, most of them **SERVICEMEN** *with kit bags, equipment, etc.*

MRS GRAY *moves into the compartment.* **MAINWARING** *catches up and follows in as well.*

MAINWARING Look, do you mind making room for this lady.

MRS GRAY *is trying to put her case on the rack.*

Here, let me help you.

PORTER'S VOICE Hurry along, please—hurry along.

MAINWARING *struggles to get the case on the rack.*

MRS GRAY Hurry up, or you'll be coming to London, too.

She bundles him out and shuts the door.

MAINWARING *(on the platform)* How do I get in touch with you?

MRS GRAY You won't be able to.

MAINWARING You'll write, won't you?

MRS GRAY Maybe—after a while—I don't know.

PORTER'S VOICE Stand clear, please.

The **PORTER**'s *whistle sounds.*

MAINWARING But, please, you must—promise me you'll write.

MRS GRAY Very well—I promise.

The train whistle blows and there is the sound of the train moving off.

The lights fade to a spot on **MAINWARING**.

MAINWARING Please make it soon.

MRS GRAY *(more distant)* Goodbye, George.

MAINWARING Goodbye, Fiona... Bye...

> *Steam blows across him as the sound of the train recedes into the distance and the lights fade to blackout.*

THE GODIVA
AFFAIR

THE GODIVA AFFAIR

Original television transmission by the BBC on 6th December, 1974 with the following cast of characters:

CAPTAIN MAINWARING	Arthur Lowe
SERGEANT WILSON	John Le Mesurier
LANCE CORPORAL JONES	Clive Dunn
PRIVATE FRAZER	John Laurie
PRIVATE GODFREY	Arnold Ridley
PRIVATE PIKE	Ian Lavender
CHIEF WARDEN HODGES, ARP warden	Bill Pertwee
PRIVATE CHEESEMAN	Talfryn Thomas
VICAR	Frank Williams
MR YEATMAN, the Verger	Edward Sinclair
MRS PIKE	Janet Davies
MRS FOX	Pamela Cundell
MR GORDON, the Town Clerk	Eric Longworth
PRIVATE DAY	Peter Honri
WAITRESS	Rosemary Faith
PRIVATE SPONGE	Colin Bean
PRIVATE HANCOCK	George Hancock
PLATOON	Michael Moore, Desmond Cullum-Jones Freddie White, Freddie Wiles, Evan Ross, Leslie Noyes, Roger Bourne, Hugh Cecil
YOUNG GIRLS	Penny Lambirth, Yasmin Lascelles, Elaina Grand, Belinda Lee

CHARACTERS

CAPTAIN MAINWARING
SERGEANT WILSON
LANCE CORPORAL JONES
PRIVATE FRAZER
PRIVATE GODFREY
PRIVATE CHEESEMAN
PRIVATE PIKE
PRIVATE SPONGE
PRIVATE HANCOCK
PRIVATE DAY
MRS FOX
WAITRESS
CHIEF WARDEN HODGES, ARP Warden
MR YEATMAN, the Verger
VICAR
MR GORDON, the Town Clerk
MRS PIKE
OTHER MEMBERS OF THE PLATOON
GIRLS IN SWIMMING COSTUMES

The action takes place in Walmington-on-Sea on the south coast of England

Time—1940

Scene One

In the Office and the Church Hall.

MAINWARING *is in the office talking to* **PRIVATE HANCOCK,** *who has a rifle and affixed bayonet.*

MAINWARING Right, Hancock, you are to stay on guard outside this door and let no-one through. Understand?

HANCOCK Right, sir. Let no-one through.

MAINWARING Maximum security. Is that clear? Maximum security.

HANCOCK Yes, Captain Mainwaring, maximum security.

MAINWARING *goes through the door into the hall. The lights go down in the office.*

MAINWARING Right, men, this is top secret. Put the blackouts up. Private Woods and Meadows on guard outside the main doors. No-one is to enter. I don't care who they are. *(He knocks on the office door)* All clear out there, Hancock?

HANCOCK All clear, sir.

MAINWARING *comes down to centre of the hall.*

MAINWARING Good. *(Pause)* Right, Jones, all clear!

JONES *(offstage)* Right you are, sir.

The door at the side of the stage opens. **JONES, FRAZER, PIKE** *and* **GODFREY, CHEESEMAN** *and* **SPONGE** *file on. They are dressed as Morris Dancers, with* **PRIVATE DAY** *who plays the concertina or recorder.*

MAINWARING Excellent turnout, men, excellent!

JONES Permission to speak, sir! Aren't you going to wear your attire?

MAINWARING Not at the moment. I'll just wear the hat. Now pay attention. The reasons I have taken all these precautions to keep this secret is because no-one must see this dance until it's perfect, otherwise we might look like a bunch of idiots! *(He puts on his hat—his bowler hat which is adorned with ribbons and rosettes)*

FRAZER Captain Mainwaring, if l can have a word. As a Scot I must say that I feel a right Jessie dressed up in this pansy Sassenach get-up!

JONES They are not pansy! This is our English national dress.

FRAZER English national dress, rubbish! Cricket clothes, with bells and ribbons on.

MAINWARING All right, Frazer, you can sneer, but if you care to work it out, it's a costume that sums up the English character pretty well. Clean white cricket flannels that stand for fair play and sportsmanship. The bowler hat that stands for respectability and clear thinking. And the ribbons and bells for just a touch of frivolity.

GODFREY Beautifully put, Captain Mainwaring.

JONES General Kitchener liked a touch of frivolity, sir. He used to wear great long—

MAINWARING All right, Jones, we've no time for that now.

JONES Pity, it was a good story.

MAINWARING *(shouting)* Hurry up, Wilson!

WILSON *(offstage left)* Do you think that someone could open the door for me, sir?

MAINWARING Go and help him, Pike. *(To the others)* Now I don't want to take too long over this rehearsal, we've got a full training programme ahead of us tonight. Right, Private Day. Stand by with your concertina. *(Or recorder)*

DAY Right you are, sir.

PRIVATE DAY *plays a chord.*

MAINWARING Good.

WILSON *comes through the door wearing a hobby horse with a skirt and little legs which are the wrong way round. He has some trouble getting through the door.*

WILSON This is really most awkward, sir.

MAINWARING You'll soon get used to it.

JONES Permission to speak, sir. Sergeant Wilson is not looking like a normal man, his little legs are going in the wrong direction.

MAINWARING Do try and sort yourself out, Wilson. *(He pulls the legs the right way round)* As you know, men, we only need another two thousand pounds to reach our target, which is to buy a Spitfire. Now, during the whole of next week, everyone in Walmington-on-Sea will be doing their utmost to raise the money. The grand climax will be the procession next Saturday afternoon: that is when we will perform our dance. Sergeant Wilson will collect the money from the crowd.

WILSON Excuse me, sir. I don't think I like the idea of asking strangers for money.

MAINWARING It's perfectly simple. All you have to do is to gallop the horse, try to make it look as life-like as possible, then you weave in and out of the dancers. Then you weave round the edge of the crowd, pull open the horse's mouth for them to put the money in, and while you're doing it, make jocular remarks.

WILSON What sort of jocular remarks?

MAINWARING Oh I don't know. You could say: "Har, har, har, give 'til it hurts. Har, har, har". Try that.

WILSON *(pathetically)* Har, har, har, give 'til it hurts. Har, har, har.

JONES If we're going to collect two thousand pounds he'll have to be a bit more jocular than that, sir.

GODFREY I don't think he can afford to be too jocular, otherwise people will think he's being over-familiar.

PIKE I've got it. Why can't he say: "We need Spitfires to beat the Hun, put money in my mouth and it goes to my tum".

FRAZER Rubbish. All he's got to do is to wave his stick at the crowd and shout: "Give us some money or I'll bash your head in".

WILSON Oh really, sir, couldn't you get someone else to do the horse?

MAINWARING No, you are going to do the horse, and that is an order. Right. Form up. Sponge, give the book to Sergeant Wilson.

SPONGE *hands the book to* **WILSON**. *They form up in two lines facing each other.* **FRAZER** *opposite* **JONES**, **PIKE** *opposite* **GODFREY** *and* **SPONGE** *opposite* **CHEESEMAN**. **WILSON** *sits down awkwardly, he tries crossing his legs but can't.*

Now where did we get to last time?

JONES I was having trouble with my whiffling, sir.

MAINWARING Oh yes. Whiffling. Now I think it is very important that we should fully understand the meaning of these movements. Read out the bit about whiffling, Wilson.

WILSON Whiffling. Right, whiffling. *(Reading)* 'The movements with the whiffling stick represent frightening the evil spirits away."

MAINWARING There you are.

PIKE Away from what, Mr Mainwaring?

MAINWARING This is a fertility dance, Pike.

GODFREY I don't think my sister Dolly would approve of that sort of thing, sir.

FRAZER Ah, you silly old fool. The whole idea of this dance is to encourage the crops to grow. It's danced every Spring by the young fertile men of the village.

JONES Well, it's not much good us doing it, is it?

FRAZER You speak for yourself.

JONES *and* **FRAZER** *face up to each other.*

MAINWARING All right, that will do.

JONES Permission to speak, sir. I do not want to stand opposite Private Frazer when he is whiffling.

MAINWARING Why not?

JONES Well sir, I have faced whirling Dervishes, and I have faced charging Fuzzie Wuzzies, but I do not want to face Private Frazer when he is waving his whiffling stick. He's got a mad look in his eyes.

FRAZER Mad? Mad? My eyes are perfectly sane. Captain Mainwaring, would you say that I had mad eyes?

MAINWARING Well, er...no...not really mad.

FRAZER There you are you see.

MAINWARING What's next, Wilson?

WILSON The bean sprouting.

MAINWARING Ah yes, the bean sprouting. Come here, Pike. Now you tap twice on the ground, so... *(He taps* **PIKE***'s stick)* ...then you shout, "Woa!" and leap up in the air; this represents the beans growing.

PIKE How high do you want us to leap, Mr Mainwaring?

MAINWARING As high as a bean grows.

CHEESEMAN I had some last year that grew to eight feet.

GODFREY I don't think I could quite manage that, sir.

SPONGE I can leap high, Mr Mainwaring. How's this? *(Shouting)* "Whoa!" *(He gives a terrific leap in the air and lands with a crash)*

MAINWARING Yes, yes.

WILSON I think we ought to be a bit careful, sir. The vicar's got dry rot in the hall. *(He stands up and, during the following, keeps bumping into people)*

MAINWARING Perhaps you're right, Wilson. We won't do the leap. Now we'll go through the whole thing from the start. Ready, Private Day?

DAY Ready! *(He gives a blast on his concertina or recorder)*

MAINWARING Oh, just before we start. I'd better make sure that your bells are working properly. Left legs.

They all shake their left legs.

Right legs.

They all shake their right legs.

That the best you can do, Godfrey?

GODFREY A touch of rheumatics, I'm afraid, sir.

MAINWARING *gives* **GODFREY** *a look of despair.*

WILSON *(bumping into* **MAINWARING***)* I'm terribly sorry, sir!

MAINWARING Look do try and keep that animal under control, Wilson.

WILSON He's not used to this type of work you see.

MAINWARING Right, off we go.

PRIVATE DAY *begins to play the concertina/recorder.*

ALL DANCERS One, two, three, four, five, six, seven, eight.

PRIVATE DAY *plays a traditional Morris Dancing air. They move back. They move forwards. They circle clockwise. They circle anti-clockwise. They whiffle. They do bean sprouting. They whiffle again and finish. All the time* **MAINWARING** *is calling the moves. At the end of the dance* **FRAZER** *is carried away with his whiffling hitting sticks hard with* **JONES** *with a mad look in his eye.*

Excellent, men. I'm very proud of you. Right, now take a break and change into your uniforms. Jones.

The platoon exit, with the exception of **JONES**, **WILSON** *and* **MAINWARING**. *Costume change:* **FRAZER**, **GODFREY**, **PIKE** *and* **CHEESEMAN** *first as they are needed in Scene Two. Dressing gowns to go over the top of civilian clothes for* **FRAZER**, **GODFREY** *and* **PIKE** *and an overcoat and hat for* **CHEESEMAN**. *The rest of the platoon change back into uniform.*

JONES Yes, sir.

MAINWARING *takes him aside.*

MAINWARING Now look, Jones, what's the matter with you? All that nonsense about Frazer hitting you with his stick. That's not like you at all.

JONES I know, sir. I'm afraid I cannot cover it up any longer. I am in a highly nervous state.

MAINWARING What's the matter?

JONES Well, sir, it's er— *(Lowering his voice)* —it's er, very personal.

MAINWARING Have you got trouble at home?

JONES No sir, I've got trouble away from home.

MAINWARING You'd better come in the office.

JONES Right, thank you sir, thank you sir, oh sir could Mr Wilson come as well, sir?

MAINWARING Why?

JONES 'Cause he's a man of the world.

MAINWARING Oh, very well. Wilson.

WILSON Yes, sir.

MAINWARING Office.

WILSON Do you want me to walk or gallop?

MAINWARING Just get in the office!

The lights fade down on the hall. Background music as necessary.

Scene Two

In the Office. Immediately following.

The lights come up in the office on **MAINWARING, JONES**
and **WILSON**.

MAINWARING Sit down, Jones,

JONES Thank you, sir, thank you.

> **JONES** *sits.* **MAINWARING** *sits behind the desk.* **WILSON**
> *stands at the top of the desk. The horse's head goes right
> across the desk.*

MAINWARING Now, Jones.

The horse's head blocks his view of **JONES**.

Get that thing off the desk, Wilson.

WILSON I'm sorry, sir. I can't help it, it sort of sticks out.

MAINWARING Well, take it off.

> **WILSON** *takes off the horse.*

Now come along, Jones.

JONES This really is very delicate, sir, you see it's er—Mrs Fox!

MAINWARING Mrs Fox?

JONES Yes, sir. She's a widow lady and we both have a certain
arrangement. For some time now we've been walking out.

MAINWARING Walking out where?

JONES All over the place. You see I take a couple of chops round
to her house every Saturday night, she cooks them and we
have supper together.

MAINWARING I see. *(He looks at* **WILSON***)* You're not the only
member of this platoon who has that arrangement with a
widow.

WILSON Really, sir, that was a bit below the belt.

JONES There is nothing between Mrs Fox and myself, sir. It is purely a teutonic arrangement. As I said, every Saturday night we have supper together, and listen to *In Town Tonight*. Then when the announcer says, "Carry on London", I go home.

MAINWARING I really don't see what this has got to do with me.

JONES Well sir, just lately her affections have been taken by another.

MAINWARING Who?

JONES Mr Gordon, the Town Clerk.

WILSON What, that silly old bald-headed duffer? *(He laughs)*

> **MAINWARING** *removes his hat as* **WILSON***'s laugh becomes an embarrassed one.* **MAINWARING** *gives him a glare.*

I, er—don't mean that he's a silly old duffer because he's got a bald head. He'd be a silly old duffer even if he had a full head of hair.

MAINWARING All right, Wilson. All right.

JONES Everyone knows that he is a rogue and a philanthropist. Her head has been turned by the gay life that he is showing her. Old Time dancing at Pevensey Bay, and trips to Eastbourne. What can I offer her? I'm just a simple butcher.

MAINWARING But I really don't see what I can do, Jones.

JONES I want you to speak to her for me.

MAINWARING But I couldn't possibly.

JONES But you must, sir, you must.

> *He rises and hands* **MAINWARING** *a piece of paper.*

Here, I've written down her telephone number. Don't spread it around.

MAINWARING Yes, but—

JONES Please speak to her, sir. Otherwise I shall be a broken man, and what use is a broken Lance Corporal to you?

JONES *exits.*

MAINWARING I don't know. I suppose I could speak to her. I think perhaps I ought to point out what sort of man this Town Clerk is. I'll give her a ring and arrange to meet her.

Costume change. **JONES** *changes into uniform through Scene Three and has a mac and balaclava over the top for Scene Four.*

The lights fade and the tabs close. Music fades up as necessary to cover the scene change.

Scene Three

FRAZER*'s and* GODFREY*'s,* PIKE*'s and* CHEESEMAN*'s houses at night.*

Pools of light fade up either side of stage in front of the tabs. Each side is set with chair, table, standard lamp and phone. FRAZER *and* GODFREY *are in dressing-gowns on the phone to each other.*

FRAZER Hallo, hallo, Godfrey, son, are you there?

GODFREY Yes, I'm here; I was just having my hot milk before going to bed.

FRAZER Well, it's happened. I knew it would some day.

GODFREY What has?

FRAZER Mainwaring has succumbed to the lure of the flesh. Did you hear what I said, Godfrey son? The flesh, the flesh!

GODFREY Oh please don't keep repeating that word, my sister Dolly might hear you. Anyhow, I refuse to believe a word of it.

FRAZER I tell you, I heard it with my own ears. It just so happened that I was passing the office door and I heard him speaking to this woman.

GODFREY Er—what woman?

FRAZER Mrs Fox. That fine big widow woman.

GODFREY But Mr Mainwaring is a pillar of respectability.

FRAZER It's men like him that are the worst. Always looking down his nose at other folk, and all the time, deep inside, lust, lust, sheer naked lust. I tell you, the fires of hell are lying in wait for him. He's doomed. Doomed!

GODFREY I think the whole thing's nonsense.

FRAZER Nonsense, is it? I heard him arrange to meet this woman at the Marigold Tea Rooms tomorrow morning at ten thirty. If you don't believe me, come and see for yourself.

GODFREY Very well, I'll come. Just to prove that you're wrong.

FRAZER Right, I'll see you there, and don't forget it's your turn to pay for the coffee.

The lights fade on FRAZER *and* GODFREY.

FRAZER *and* GODFREY *exit to remove their dressing-gowns, having civilian clothes underneath for Scene Four.* PIKE *and* CHEESEMAN *enter.*

Music as necessary to cover the change.

Pools of light come up on CHEESEMAN *and* PIKE. CHEESEMAN *is dressed in a mac and hat private-eye style.* PIKE *is on the other end of the line. He is dressed in his dressing-gown.*

CHEESEMAN Hallo, hallo. Listen, Pikey, I've got to speak to you. It's very important, boyo.

PIKE What do you want to ring me up at this time of night for? Mum's furious.

MRS PIKE *(offstage)* Who's that on the phone, Frank? It's not a girl, is it?

PIKE No, mum, it's Mr Cheeseman.

MRS PIKE *(offstage)* How dare he ring you up in the middle of the night? Tell him to go away.

PIKE It's only ten o'clock, Mum.

MRS PIKE *(offstage)* I don't care. You should be in bed. And don't forget to clean your teeth.

PIKE Mum says I've got to go to bed and clean my teeth.

CHEESEMAN Oh yes. Clean your teeth. They're very important. I just want a bit of information. What time does Mainwaring go for his morning coffee?

PIKE Ten thirty every morning at the Marigold Tea Rooms, regular as clockwork. Why?

CHEESEMAN Well, I have it from a very reliable source that Captain Mainwaring is meeting a certain lady there.

PIKE Oh no, Mr Mainwaring doesn't know certain ladies. He's married.

CHEESEMAN Well she's not so much a lady, see, she's sort of... well you know, very much... *(He gestures with his hands)* Anyhow, I write this gossip column for the *Eastgate Gazette*, "Whispers from Walmington". Oh yes, indeed, I can see it now. "What certain local bank manager's name is linked with a certain widow lady X?"

PIKE No, no, I'm sure you've got it all wrong.

CHEESEMAN My information is that he's besotted with her, boyo, besotted!

PIKE Hey, like in that film *Rain*. This clergyman was besotted with a girl called Sadie Thompson. Well, being a clergyman, he wasn't allowed to be besotted, so in the end he walked into the sea. Here, you don't think Captain Mainwaring will walk into the sea, do you? If he does, he'll have to walk miles. The tide's out tomorrow morning!

Blackout. Music over the scene change. The pools of light fade.

Scene Four

Marigold Tea Rooms.

The front tabs open and the lights come up.

FRAZER *and* **GODFREY** *are sitting at a table in the corner. They are both dressed in civilian clothes.* **CHEESEMAN** *is sitting at another table behind a newspaper, still in mac and hat.* **JONES** *is sitting at a table, behind a newspaper. He is wearing a balaclava, bowler hat and mac.*

GODFREY I'm sorry, Mr Frazer, Mr Mainwaring is a respectable married man. I refuse to believe that he's capable of such a thing.

FRAZER You know your trouble, Godfrey, you live in a fool's paradise. I tell you—

MAINWARING *and* **WILSON** *enter.*

Shhhh! Here he is.

MAINWARING *nods at* **FRAZER** *and* **GODFREY**.

MAINWARING I had hoped that we'd have the place to ourselves, Wilson.

WILSON I shouldn't worry, sir. No-one knows why you're meeting Mrs Fox.

MAINWARING Look, it doesn't do for a man in my position to be seen in a public place with a flashy woman like Mrs Fox. In a small town like this, tongues wag, you know, tongues wag.

WILSON I'm sure no-one's the slightest bit interested, sir. Where shall we sit?

MAINWARING I shall sit here. *(He points to a table downstage centre)* You go and sit on your own. *(He puts his bowler hat on his seat)*

JONES *(lowering his newspaper)* Psst, psst! Mr Mainwaring.

MAINWARING Good-morning. Is that you, Jones?

JONES You won't let me down, will you, sir?

MAINWARING Why on earth are you dressed like that?

JONES I'm in disguise, sir. I don't want anybody to recognize me.

MRS FOX *enters.*

MAINWARING *sits on his hat.* JONES *disappears behind his newspaper.*

MRS FOX Yoo, hoo! Mr Mainwaring! —Morning, Mr Frazer, Mr Godfrey; morning, Mr Wilson.

They all react.

Hallo, Mr Mainwaring, sorry I'm late.

MAINWARING *(standing)* Please sit down, Mrs Fox.

MRS FOX I'm usually on time when I meet a gentleman friend, but today...

MAINWARING Sit down, please.

He pushes her to her chair.

FRAZER Did you see that, Godfrey! Did you see the way he handled her?

MAINWARING *picks his hat up and punches it back into shape and settles it on a shelving unit behind in full view of the audience.*

MRS FOX *(settling down)* Well, this is cosy...

The WAITRESS *comes to the table.*

WAITRESS Good-morning, sir.

MAINWARING Ah, good-morning. Two coffees please.

WAITRESS Aren't you having coffee with your friend Mr Wilson this morning?

MAINWARING No, I'm not, I'm having this lady with my coffee! I mean I'm having coffee with this lady. Two coffees please.

WAITRESS I see.

She giggles and goes. PIKE *comes in.*

MAINWARING Now Mrs Fox. I have, er—asked you to meet me here today because—

PIKE *approaches behind the shelving unit and leans on* MAINWARING*'s hat, flattening it.*

PIKE Excuse me, Mr Mainwaring.

MAINWARING What do you want, boy? *(He punches his hat back into shape again)*

PIKE Mrs Mainwaring's on the phone.

MAINWARING What! Oh yes. Well, tell her I'll ring her back later.

PIKE Ring her back later. Right. Hallo, Mrs Fox.

MRS FOX Hallo, dear.

PIKE *exits.*

MAINWARING Well now, Mrs Fox. I've asked you to meet me here today, because I have to speak to you on a very delicate matter.

MRS FOX *(leaning forward)* Yes?

MAINWARING I find these things concerned with emotions very difficult to discuss.

MRS FOX You needn't be shy with me, Mr Mainwaring.

MAINWARING Well now the fact is, Mrs Fox, you are a very attractive woman.

MRS FOX And you're a very attractive man, Mr Mainwaring.

MAINWARING I can't see what that's got to do with it.

MRS FOX Ooooh you are! You are!

MAINWARING What I'm trying to say is, you have had Mr Jones as an admirer for some years, and now, of course, you have another.

MRS FOX Oh, Mr Mainwaring.

She grabs his hand.

FRAZER Did you see that! Did you see the way he manhandled her?

GODFREY Oh dear. Perhaps we'd better go.

CHEESEMAN *is writing.* **WILSON** *is looking.* **MAINWARING** *snatches his hand away.*

MAINWARING I realize, of course, that, being a public figure, this other man must seem very attractive to you.

MRS FOX Oh, he is—he is!

MAINWARING Jones, on the other hand, is just a simple butcher, but a fine figure of a man, Mrs Fox. A full head of grey, distinguished hair. Your other admirer is, not to put too fine a point on it, bald.

MRS FOX Well, Mr Mainwaring, you know what they say about bald-headed men.

MAINWARING *(interested)* No, what do they say?

PIKE *enters.*

The point is, Mrs Fox, Jones is a very loyal member of my platoon and I don't want him hurt.

MRS FOX We won't hurt him, Mr Mainwaring.

MAINWARING *(after a pause)* We!

MRS FOX He can have Mondays and Saturdays, and you can have Tuesdays and Fridays.

MAINWARING *(flustered)* Madam, I'm talking about Mr Gordon, the Town Clerk.

MRS FOX Well, he can have Wednesdays.

PIKE Excuse me, sir.

Again he leans on the bowler hat and flattens it.

MAINWARING What is it, boy? *(He punches his hat back into shape again)*

PIKE I'm sorry to disturb you again, Mr Mainwaring, but Mrs Mainwaring is on the phone again. I told her you were busy having coffee with Mrs Fox but she insists on speaking to you.

MAINWARING You stupid boy!

Blackout. The tabs close.

Scene Five

The Office and the Church Hall.

The tabs open. The hall is in darkness and the **VICAR,**
VERGER *and* **MR GORDON,** *the Town Clerk, are sitting
at a table in the middle of the hall, while* **HODGES** *is
standing by a vaulting horse in front of the table. They
are in a freeze.*

The lights come up to reveal **MAINWARING** *and* **WILSON**
in the office.

MAINWARING I tell you, Wilson, I've never been so shocked
in all my life. That woman, that dreadful woman, actually
thought that I had amorous intentions towards her.

WILSON Oh dear! How awfully embarrassing for you, sir.

MAINWARING And to make matters worse, when my wife phoned
up, that stupid boy Pike told her I was having coffee with
Mrs Fox.

WILSON Oh dear!

MAINWARING All hell let loose when I got home. Elizabeth
refused to listen to my explanations, and look what she
did to my tie. *(He pulls his tie out. It has been cut short at
the ends)* She rang me up twelve times at the bank today.
Now if she rings tonight I want you to tell her I'm not here.
You understand?

WILSON Yes, I understand all right, sir.

JONES enters through the outside door.

JONES Evening, Mr Wilson, evening, sir. I want to thank you
for speaking to Mrs Fox like that, I'm sure you had a great
effect on her.

WILSON Yes, he really did.

FRAZER, PIKE, GODFREY, CHEESEMAN *and several other members of the platoon enter from outside.* FRAZER *is carrying the Lewis gun.*

FRAZER Captain Mainwaring, we cannay get into the hall, the doors are locked.

PIKE Yeah! Mr Hodges shouted at us to go away.

MAINWARING As if I haven't got enough to put up with as it is. *(He crosses to the door to the hall and tries the handle. It is locked)* It's locked, Wilson.

WILSON It is Hodges' night to have the hall, sir.

MAINWARING I know that, but there's no need for him to lock the door. All right, Frazer, put the Lewis gun on the desk. I'll start the lecture. *(He crosses to the desk)* Now my subject tonight, men, is stripping down.

The lights fade on the office and the cast freeze. The lights come up on the hall. A vaulting-horse stands in the middle (if a vaulting-horse is not available the edge of a table will do).

HODGES All right, girls, you can come out.

Five girls in swimming costumes come through the door at the side of the stage.

Line up, girls.

They line up.

HODGES Right. What do you think then, Mr Town Clerk?

GORDON Oh, they're very nice, they are.

VERGER I quite agree with you. What do you think, Your Reverence?

VICAR Look, can we get on please. I've got a very busy evening ahead of me.

HODGES *crosses to the* **VICAR**, *nudges him and leers.*

HODGES *(whispering)* I wouldn't mind having a busy evening with this lot, eh?

VICAR Just explain to the girls what we want, Mr Hodges.

HODGES Right. Now girls, as you know, we have got you here tonight so that we can choose one of you to play the part of Lady Godiva in the procession next week.

GORDON Can we have the first girl on the horse, please?

HODGES Right, girls. On the horse.

The girls move to the horse. The lights fade on the hall and the cast freeze.

The lights come up on the office. MAINWARING *and the rest of the platoon are gathered round the Lewis gun on the table.* PIKE *and* WILSON *are by the door.* PIKE *has his eye to the keyhole.*

MAINWARING Right, Jones, I want you to show the men how to strip the Lewis gun down in two minutes, and I shall time you. Are you ready?

JONES Yes sir, yes sir.

MAINWARING *(looking at his watch)* Strip.

JONES *starts on the gun.* PIKE *straightens.*

PIKE *(whispering in* WILSON*'s ear)* Uncle Arthur.

WILSON What is it?

PIKE The hall's full of naked girls.

WILSON Don't be stupid, Frank. Pay attention to the lecture.

PIKE It's true, come and have a look for yourself, c'mon.

He pushes WILSON *down to the keyhole.*

WILSON Oh good heavens!

PIKE Shall we tell Mr Mainwaring?

WILSON Well I, er...

The phone rings.

MAINWARING Answer the phone, will you, Wilson, please.

WILSON Yes, sir.

MAINWARING Hurry up, Jones, you've only got another thirty seconds.

WILSON *picks up the phone.*

WILSON Hallo. Oh good-evening. Just a minute. *(He puts his hand over the mouthpiece; whispering to* **MAINWARING***)* It's Mrs Mainwaring, sir.

MAINWARING I told you to tell her I wasn't here.

WILSON Sorry, sir. *(Into the phone)* I'm afraid he's gone out for a little while.

MRS FOX *suddenly appears through the outside door.*

MRS FOX *(in a loud voice)* Yoohoo, Mr Mainwaring, I'm here.

MAINWARING Oh no! *(He grabs the phone and hangs up)* How dare you burst in on one of my lectures like this.

MRS FOX Oh I'm sorry, just on my way to the hall. Excuse me, boys. *(She pushes her way through the crowd. She is carrying a small case. She knocks on the door)* Mr Gordon, let me in, it's only little me!

GORDON, *the Town Clerk, opens the door of the office.*

GORDON Good-evening, my dear. You're just in time. Come in.

JONES *(agitated)* Mr Mainwaring! Mr Mainwaring! He's at it again; what's he doing?

MAINWARING I don't know, Jones, but I'll soon find out.

MAINWARING *goes into the hall, followed by the others.*

(beside himself) What is the meaning of this?

HODGES Buzz off, Napoleon. This is my night to have the hall.

MAINWARING How dare you! How dare you have naked girls in my HQ? I'm appalled at you, Vicar. Wilson! Wilson! Don't keep staring at the girls. Cover them up.

WILSON What with?

MAINWARING *(to* **PIKE***)* Come away, boy.

VICAR Don't be absurd. All this fuss over a few silly girls.

VERGER Yes, if the vicar wants to have silly girls in his hall, that's his affair.

MRS FOX Mr Gordon! Shall I change into my swimming costume now?

FRAZER God, I don't think I could stand the shock.

GORDON Yes, my dear. Go and get changed.

JONES Mr Mainwaring, stop him, he's doing it again, Mr Mainwaring. Stop him! Stop him!

MAINWARING Be quiet, Jones. Hodges, I demand an explanation of this.

HODGES Keep your hair on, we're just choosing a girl to play the part of Lady Godiva in the procession next Saturday.

MAINWARING Lady Godiva!

HODGES Yeah, Lady Godiva, and it's much better than your silly Morris Dancing.

JONES Our Morris Dancing is not silly.

MAINWARING Just a minute, Mr Town Clerk. Do I understand that one of those young ladies is going to ride—er—naked, through the streets of Walmington?

GORDON Yes, it's a tribute to the brave City of Coventry. The girl won't be bare, of course, she'll wear *(he smacks his lips)* —fleshings.

MAINWARING Fleshings!

WILSON It's all right, sir, they're all-over body tights and perfectly respectable.

MAINWARING All-over body tights!

HODGES Yes. Lovely. We're not living in Victorian times, you know.

MRS FOX Mr Gordon, do you think I might have a little word in your ear?

JONES He's doing it again, sir, stop him, sir, stop him.

MAINWARING Yes all right, Jones, now look here, er...

GORDON Now wait a minute, Captain Mainwaring, I think we have a solution. You don't want one of those young girls as Lady Godiva. Now it's just been pointed out to me that Lady Godiva Leofric was, in fact, a woman of more er, mature years. So in the course of historical accuracy, I suggest that Lady Godiva should be Mrs Fox.

Uproar from the girls and the platoon.

Quiet, please! Mrs Fox will be perfectly respectable, covered from top to toe in *(he smacks his lips)* fleshings, and wearing a wig of long golden tresses.

FRAZER Tsh. You'll never cover her with golden tresses. You'll need a bell tent.

Blackout. The tabs close. Music as required to cover the scene change.

Scene Six

In the Office.

The tabs open, the music fades down and the lights come up on the office.

MAINWARING *is on the phone.*

MAINWARING Yes, Elizabeth... No, Elizabeth. I keep telling you that I had nothing whatsoever to do with the choosing of Mrs Fox as Lady Godiva.

WILSON *comes in from the hall.*

Yes, dear... No, dear. It was the Town Clerk's decision. He thought it would be better for the part to be taken by a woman of more mature...well ample proportions. Yes, dear, I realize that you have more ample proportions than Mrs Fox. But then, you're not Lady Godiva, are you? ...Hallo, hallo, dear? *(He hangs up and gives* **WILSON** *a sickly grin)* Just chatting to the little woman.

WILSON Oh I see, what little woman?

MAINWARING My wife, of course.

JONES *comes in through the outside door.*

JONES I've lost her, Mr Mainwaring. Ever since the Town Clerk chose Mrs Fox for Lady Godiva, her head's been turned completely, right round.

WILSON I'm sorry, I'm so sorry, Jonesey.

MAINWARING You see this is what happens, Wilson, when women come into men's affairs. The whole platoon has been thrown completely sideways.

PIKE *and* **MRS PIKE** *come in through the outside door.*

PIKE No, Mum, no, you can't come in now, Mum, we're just going to go on parade.

MRS PIKE Get out of my way, Frank. *(She nods to* **MAINWARING***)* Goodevening, Mr Mainwaring. Arthur, what's this I hear about Mrs Fox being chosen as Lady Godiva?

WILSON It was really nothing to do with me, Mavis.

MRS PIKE Well you were there.

WILSON Well I was, yes, sort of standing around.

MRS PIKE A woman like Mrs Fox! I'm much slimmer than she is. I mean, what's wrong with my figure?

WILSON What, er, nothing, nothing at all.

MRS PIKE I've got nice legs, haven't I? Haven't I got nice legs?

WILSON Yes, awfully nice.

MAINWARING You don't want to play Lady Godiva, Mrs Pike.

MRS PIKE But I would have liked to have been asked.

MAINWARING Have you considered the affect on your son, his mother riding through the streets, clad in nothing but—but...

PIKE *(smacking his lips mimicking* **MR GORDON***)* Fleshings.

MAINWARING Well I know how I would feel if it was anyone close to me. So my advice to you is to let sleeping dogs lie.

Blackout. The tabs close. Music as required to cover the scene change.

Scene Seven

The Church Hall.

The tabs open, the lights come up full on the hall and the music fades out.

MAINWARING *and his men are in the hall. They are dressed as Morris Dancers.*

MAINWARING Right men, are you all ready? Now as soon as the procession has gone past, Jones will open the door, we will burst out into the street and perform the dance.

GODFREY I'm not awfully good at bursting out, Mr Mainwaring.

MAINWARING You'll just have to do the best you can, Godfrey.

There is the sound of a band and crowds cheering. **PIKE** *pulls the curtain aside.*

PIKE Mr Mainwaring, the procession is coming now.

MAINWARING Good, good. Stand by.

MAINWARING *turns and tussles with* **WILSON**'s *horse that is in his way.*

MRS FOX *bursts in. She is wearing only a coat and her hair is all over the place.*

JONES Mrs Fox. What happened?

MRS FOX Mr Jones! Mr Jones!

JONES What's the matter? What's the matter?

MRS FOX *(in tears)* It was terrible, terrible.

JONES Now don't you upset yourself. *(He puts his arm round her)* There, there, you're safe with your little Jack now, just tell me what's the matter.

The music gets louder.

MAINWARING There's no time for all that, Jones.

MRS FOX *(sobbing)* I was going to change in a room in the
Town Hall, and I left my fleshings and wig on a chair. Well,
I went out for a minute and when I got back they were gone.
Gone! Gone! Gone!

FRAZER What a pity! It doesn't look as if we're going to get to
see Lady Godiva after all.

MAINWARING Never mind, it's up to us now.

MAINWARING *pulls* JONES *away from comforting* MRS
FOX.

That's enough of that, Jones. Get ready to open the door.

He pushes JONES *towards the door.* PIKE *pulls the curtain
aside.*

PIKE Hey, Mr Mainwaring, there is a Lady Godiva.

WILSON Oh Lord, not Mavis.

MAINWARING *pushes to the door.*

MAINWARING I wish you'd keep that woman under control,
Wilson.

JONES No, Mr Mainwaring, don't look, sir, please don't look.

MAINWARING Get out of the way, Jones.

MAINWARING *pulls the curtain to one side and looks.
He gives a low moan and faints into* JONES *arms.*

PIKE Hey, it's Mrs Mainwaring.

JONES *cradles* MAINWARING *in his arms.*

JONES Speak to me, sir, speak to me. Poor Mr Mainwaring,
he'll never get over it.

FRAZER Ay no, and neither will the horse.

Blackout. The tabs close.

THE FLORAL DANCE

THE FLORAL DANCE

CHARACTERS

CAPTAIN MAINWARING
SERGEANT WILSON
LANCE CORPORAL JONES
PRIVATE FRAZER
PRIVATE GODFREY
PRIVATE WALKER
MRS FOX
CHIEF WARDEN HODGES, ARP Warden
MR YEATMAN, the Verger
VICAR
MRS PIKE
OTHER MEMBERS OF THE PLATOON
MRS HART
WARDENS
LADIES

The action takes place in Walmington-on-Sea on the south coast of England

Time—1940

We have included "The Floral Dance" sketch because it was so successful in the production at The Shaftesbury Theatre, London, and was also performed by the Dad's Army team when they appeared in the Royal Command Variety Performance. If the length of the entertainment permits, it makes a wonderful finish to the first or second half of the show and includes a larger cast of Wardens and Ladies.

Scene One

In front of the tabs.

MAINWARING *and* **HODGES** *enter.*

MAINWARING No, no, certainly not. I've never heard of anything so outrageous in all my life.

HODGES Why should you be in charge of the choir any more than me, what do you know about music?

MAINWARING Now look here, Hodges. For the last time I'm telling you that this choir is my idea, and I'm conducting it.

HODGES Listen, Napoleon, you asked for some Ladies. I'm bringing 'em along, so why can't I conduct?

MAINWARING Because most of the choir come from my platoon and they're all men.

HODGES I've only got your word for that, mate.

MAINWARING How dare you!

HODGES Those wounded soldiers don't want to look at a lot of old men, they like to see pretty women.

MAINWARING We'll toss for it. *(He produces a coin)* Heads I conduct the choir, tails you conduct it.

HODGES Oh, all right.

MAINWARING *tosses the coin.*

MAINWARING Heads! I conduct the choir.

HODGES Best out of three.

Blackout.

Scene Two

The Church Hall.

The tabs go up on the Church hall.

WILSON *marches on the platoon.*

WILSON Platoon, halt! Now just get into a choir arrangement.

JONES Right, you heard what the sergeant said. Into a choir arrangement at the double.

The platoon take their places.

The **VICAR** *and* **VERGER** *enter with* **MRS HART**, **MRS PIKE** *and* **MRS FOX**.

VERGER Left, right, left, right.

VICAR Oh, don't be silly, Mr Yeatman. They're not soldiers, just take your places, ladies.

The ladies take their places.

HODGES *marches on the* **WARDENS**.

HODGES Left, right, left, right, halt. Into position please, ladies and gentlemen.

The **WARDENS** *don't move.*

(to **WILSON***)* You'll notice that I don't have to bawl and shout to keep my people in order. I dominate them by the power of my personality.

WILSON It doesn't seem to be working awfully well.

The **WARDENS** *still haven't moved.*

HODGES *(shouting)* Will you get in position.

The **WARDENS** *take their places.* **HODGES** *stands in front of* **MRS FOX**.

MAINWARING *enters.*

Evening, Sir Thomas.

MAINWARING Thank you for coming along, ladies and gentlemen. As you know, we are giving this concert next Saturday night for wounded soldiers, and as quite a number of the men are from the Duke of Cornwall's Light Infantry, I have chosen the Floral Dance to open the proceedings. *(To* WILSON*)* Take your place at the piano, Wilson.

WILSON Right, sir. *(He sits at the piano; finger business)*

MAINWARING What are you doing?

WILSON Just limbering up the digits, sir.

MAINWARING You're not Charlie Kunz, you know. Mr Hodges.

HODGES Yes?

MAINWARING I don't think it's necessary to wear your steel helmet to sing in.

MRS FOX I don't mind him keeping it on. I can rest my music and things on it.

HODGES I'll take it off. Not because of what you said, but because of what she said. *(He takes it off)*

PIKE *(to* GODFREY*)* I've never seen him without his helmet before. I always thought he hadn't got a top to his head.

HODGES I heard that, you stupid, soppy-looking boy.

MRS PIKE Don't you call my son a stupid, soppy-looking boy.

HODGES Well, he is a stupid, soppy-looking boy.

MAINWARING Please, ladies and gentlemen.

MRS HART Can we get on, please.

MAINWARING Yes, of course, Mrs Hart. *(Grin business)* Now most of you know the tune. It's very simple. The first bit's nearly all one note like this. *(He la's the first few bars)* Right, Wilson, just play the tune through for them in single notes.

WILSON *plays the first few notes. Nothing happens.*

WILSON I'm afraid the note's broken, sir.

MAINWARING Well, play the next note.

WILSON That's not the right one.

MAINWARING All right then, play one like it.

WILSON There isn't one like it in this part of the keyboard.

MAINWARING Don't try and blind me with science, Wilson.

WILSON I can manage it an octave lower, sir.

MAINWARING Well, play it then.

> **WILSON** *plays the first few bars through with one finger an octave lower.*

That's it! We'll take that bit first. Are you ready? One—two...

OMNES *(singing)*
AS I WALKED HOME ON A SUMMER NIGHT
WHEN STARS IN THE HEAVENS WERE SHINING BRIGHT.

> *It is very low for them.* **MAINWARING** *stops them.*

JONES Permission to speak, sir. It's too low. I think the ladies are having a little trouble.

MAINWARING It's too low, Wilson.

WILSON All right, sir. I'll go up a bit.

MAINWARING Good. Ready, one—two...

> **WILSON** *plays it two octaves higher.*

OMNES *(singing)*
AS I WALKED HOME ON A SUMMER NIGHT
WHEN STARS IN THE HEAVENS WERE SHINING
     BRIGHT.

JONES *(speaking)* Mr Mainwaring, it's too high. The men are having a bit of trouble.

MAINWARING It's far too high, Wilson. We don't want the one below or the one up there—we want the one in the middle.

HODGES I can't stand any more of this—I'll give it to you. *(He sings)*
AS I WALKED HOME ON A SUMMER NIGHT
WHEN STARS IN THE HEAVEN WERE SHINING BRIGHT
FAR AWAY FROM THE FOOTLIGHTS GLARE
INTO THE SWEET AND SCENTED AIR
OF A QUAINT OLD CORNISH TOWN

(speaking) How's that?

JONES Rotten.

VICAR Wait a minute. *(He gets out a pitch pipe)* I'll give it to you on my little pitch pipe.

He blows it, they all "la."

MAINWARING Thank you, Vicar.

VICAR It's such a handy little thing. I carry it with me everywhere.

VERGER His Reverence uses it to tune boy scouts.

MAINWARING Right, ladies and gentlemen, we'll take it from the beginning. We want someone for the solo "Borne from afar on the gentle breeze".

JONES Permission to speak, sir. I should like to volunteer to be the one "Borne from afar on the gentle breeze".

MAINWARING I was afraid you might—all ready? One—two...

They sing the first six bars properly. When they reach the word "town" they hold the note for the next two bars and the girls harmonize.

JONES *(singing, coming in two beats too soon)*
BORNE FROM AFAR ON THE GENTLE BREEZE.

MAINWARING *(stopping him)* Jones! Jones!

The rest stop. **JONES** *still carries on.*

Stop him, someone.

HODGES Hey—hey! *(He touches* **JONES***)* Hey!

JONES Whoa-er. *(He grabs* **HODGES** *by the throat)* Oh, I'm sorry.

MAINWARING You came in too soon, Jones—try it again. From "Into the sweet and scented air".

MAINWARING This time we'll count for you, Jones. It's two-three-four-five-six-seven-eight in. From the same place. One—two...

They all sing from **"INTO THE SWEET AND SCENTED AIR".** *They break off on the word "town" and count while the girls harmonize.*

OMNES *(speaking)* Two-three-four-five-six-seven-eight in.

JONES *gives a start and comes in.*

JONES *(singing)*
BORNE FROM AFAR ON THE GENTLE BREEZE
JOINING THE MURMUR OF THE SUMMER SEAS
DISTANT TONES OF AN OLD WORLD DANCE
PLAYED BY THE VILLAGE BAND PERCHANCE

OMNES
ON THE CALM AIR CAME FLOATING DOWN, AH, AH, *(ETC)*

MAINWARING *stops them.* **WILSON** *continues to play.*

MAINWARING Thank you, Wilson.

WILSON *stops.*

Watch my stick. Not bad—not bad at all. Now, we'll take the next bit. "I thought I could hear the curious tone of the cornet, clarinet and big trombone." I think we'll split this up. Godfrey, you take the cornet and clarinet.

GODFREY Cornet and clarinet—yes, sir.

MAINWARING Frazer—big trombone.

FRAZER Ay.

MAINWARING Pike, you take the fiddle and cello.

WILSON starts to giggle.

What are you laughing at, Wilson?

WILSON Well, I was just thinking, wouldn't it be better if Walker was on the fiddle?

He laughs. The rest of the platoon stare at him in stony silence.

MAINWARING Walker, you take the big bass drum.

WALKER Right ho!

MAINWARING Now we want someone to do the euphonium.

WALKER Why don't we split it up. Jonesy can be the U, I'll be the phone, and the vicar can be the bum.

MAINWARING One more remark out of you, Walker, and I shall ask you to leave.

HODGES I'll do the euphonium.

MAINWARING Thank you, Mr Hodges. Right, are you ready?

WILSON starts.

Don't anticipate me, Wilson—watch my stick. Ready—one—two...

OMNES
I THOUGHT I COULD HEAR THE CURIOUS TONE

GODFREY
OF THE CORNET, CLARINET

FRAZER
AND BIG TROMBONE. *(YELLING)* AI!

MAINWARING *(stopping them)* Just a minute. There's no "Ai!" after "trombone", Frazer.

FRAZER I know there isn't—I just put it in. It gives a bit of guts. Washed out English tune.

MAINWARING We'll do without it, if you don't mind.

FRAZER *mutters to himself.*

From the top, once more. Watch my stick, Wilson. One—two...

OMNES
I THOUGHT I COULD HEAR THE CURIOUS TONE

GODFREY
OF THE CORNET, CLARINET

FRAZER
AND BIG TROMBONE.

PIKE
FIDDLE, CELLO

WALKER
BIG BASS DRUM

JONES
BASSOON, FLUTE

HODGES
AND EUPHONIUM

OMNES *(soft)*
FAR AWAY AS IN A TRANCE

(very loud)
I HEARD THE SOUND OF THE FLORAL DANCE

MAINWARING *falls off the podium.* **WILSON** *helps him up.*

MAINWARING Excellent—excellent. Now, we'll go straight through to the end. Pike, you take the solo. I've marked it for you. Slowly and dreamily.

PIKE Yes, Mr Mainwaring. Slowly and dreamily.

MAINWARING Are you ready? One—two...

PIKE

> I FELT SO LONELY STANDING THERE
> AND I COULD ONLY STAND AND STARE
> FOR I HAD NO BOY GIRL WITH ME
> SLOWLY I SHOULD HAVE TO...

MAINWARING *(stopping him)* Stop! Stop! Why are you singing "for I had no boy girl"?

PIKE That's what it says here, Mainwaring. For I had no boy girl with me.

MAINWARING If you're a boy, you've a girl, and if you're a girl, you've a boy. Do you follow?

PIKE Yes.

MAINWARING You stupid boy

PIKE Well, what am I then?

WALKER We're all beginning to wonder!

MAINWARING You sing girl. Now once again. One—two...

OMNES

> I FELT SO LONELY STANDING THERE *(ETC)*

They all sing right through each doing his solos— working up to a big finish. **WILSON** *goes off the end of the piano.* **MAINWARING** *falls off the podium.*

Blackout.

FURNITURE AND PROPERTY LIST

THE DEADLY ATTACHMENT

Scene One

On stage: Office
Desk. *On it:* phone
2 chairs
Cupboard. *In it:* 2 boxes of Mills bombs, detonators
Mirror on wall

Hall
Stage. *By it:* chair
Card table
Chairs
Benches
Curtains at the windows

Downstage
Desk. *On it:* phone
Chair

Personal: **Platoon**: rifles, bayonets
Walker: flat half bottle of whisky in blouse
Mainwaring: spectacles (worn throughout), paper
in pocket, swagger stick, revolver in holster

Scene Two

Set: Office
Mills bombs on desk
Mills bomb for **Pike**

Scene Three

Off stage: Lewis gun (**Frazer**)
Tommy gun (**Pike**)
Stepladder (**Sponge** and **Hancock**)

Scene Four

Scene Five

Scene Six

Scene Seven

Scene Eight

MUM'S ARMY

Scene One

Hall
Stage
Card table
Chairs
Benches
Curtains at the windows

Personal: **Mainwaring**: spectacles (worn throughout), swagger stick

Scene Two

On stage: As before

Personal: **Mrs Fox**: handbag containing card

Scene Three

On stage: As before

Personal: **Mrs Gray**: handbag

Scene Four

Strike: Paper, pencil from desk in office

Re-set: Chairs in office

Set: Vase of dahlias on desk in office

Scene Five

On stage: Café
Tables
Chairs
Newspaper for **Godfrey**

Off stage: Newspaper (**Mainwaring**)
Menu (**Waitress**)
Bill (**Waitress**)
2 cups of coffee (**Waitress**)
Small suitcase (**Walker**)

| *Personal:* | **Mrs Gray**: handbag |
| | **Godfrey:** money |

Scene Six

| *Strike:* | Tables, chairs, coffee cups |

Scene Seven

On stage:	Station Waiting-Room and Platform
	Small refreshment counter. *On it:* hot-water machine, tired looking sandwiches in cases, cups, saucers, etc.
	Table. *By it:* suitcase
	4 chairs

| *Personal:* | **Mrs Gray**: coins in handbag |

Scene Eight

On stage:	Train Compartment
	Luggage rack
	Service kitbags, equipment, etc.

THE GODIVA AFFAIR

Scene One

On stage:	Office
	Desk. *On it:* phone
	2 chairs
	Cupboard
	Mirror on wall
	Hall
	Stage
	Card table
	Chairs
	Benches
	Curtains at windows

Off stage: Rifle and bayonet (**Hancock**)
              Concertina or recorder (**Private Day**)
              Sticks (**Jones, Frazer, Pike, Godfrey, Cheeseman, Sponge**)

Personal: **Mainwaring**: spectacles (worn throughout)
              Wilson: hobby horse
              Sponge: book
              Jones: piece of paper

Scene Two

On stage: As before

Scene Three

Strike: Hobby horse from office

Set: Downstage left
        Table. *On it*: phone
        Chair
        Standard lamp

        Downstage right
        Table. *On it*: phone
        Chair
        Standard lamp

Scene Four

Strike: Tables, phone, chairs, standard lamps

Set: Tea Rooms
        6 tables
        8 chairs
        Shelving unit
        Newspapers for **Cheeseman** and **Jones**

Personal: **Cheeseman**: notepad and pencil
            Mrs Fox: handbag

Scene Five

Strike:	Tables, chairs, shelving unit, newspapers
Set:	Vaulting horse
Re-set:	Card table in the middle of the hall 3 chairs around table
Off stage:	Lewis gun (**Frazer**) Small case (**Mrs Fox**)
Personal:	**Mainwaring**: wristwatch

Scene Six

Strike:	Lewis gun and small case from office Vaulting horse from hall

Scene Seven

Check:	Window curtains are closed
Off stage:	Sticks (**Platoon**)
Personal:	**Wilson**: hobby horse

THE FLORAL DANCE

Scene One

Personal:	**Mainwaring:** coin

Scene Two

On stage:	Hall Podium Piano and stool
Personal:	**Vicar:** pitch pipes

LIGHTING PLOT

THE DEADLY ATTACHMENT

Property Fittings required: nil

Interior and exterior settings

To open. Full general lighting in church hall and office

Cue 1	**Mainwaring**: "Stupid boy!" *Bring up spot on* **Colonel**	(Page 10)
Cue 2	**Mainwaring**: "Thank you, sir." *Fade spot on* **Colonel**	(Page 11)
Cue 3	**Mainwaring** follows the men out *Fade to blackout; when ready, bring up general lighting in office for Scene Two*	(Page 12)
Cue 4	**Wilson** and **Pike** put detonators in the bombs *Fade to blackout; when ready, bring up general lighting in hall for Scene Three*	(Page 14)
Cue 5	**Mainwaring**: 'Take charge, **Wilson**." *Crossfade to the office*	(Page 20)
Cue 6	**Mainwaring**: "**Mainwaring** here!" *Bring up spot on* **Colonel**	(Page 20)
Cue 7	**Mainwaring** hangs up *Fade spot on* **Colonel**	(Page 21)
Cue 8	**Mainwaring**: "Fish and chips!" *Crossfade to the hall*	(Page 21)
Cue 9	**Walker**: "Soggy chips." *Fade to blackout; when ready, bring up general lighting in hall for Scene Four*	(Page 25)

MUM'S ARMY

Property fittings required: nil

Various interior and exterior settings

Scene One

To open : Full general lighting on church hall

Cue 2	**Wilson** goes into the hall	(Page 54)
	Blackout; when ready, bring up	
	lighting on office and church hall for	
	Scene Three	
Cue 3	**Wilson**: "...how they shape up."	(Page 58)
	Blackout; when ready, bring up	
	lighting on church hall for Scene	
	Four	
Cue 4	**Frazer**: "They're like tree trunks."	(Page 59)
	Bring up lighting on office	
Cue 5	**Mainwaring**: "...it's an order."	(Page 63)
	Fade to blackout; when ready, bring up	
	lighting on café for Scene Five	
Cue 6	**Mrs Gray** reaches for her handbag	(Page 68)
	Blackout; when ready, bring up	
	lighting on church hall for Scene Six	
Cue 7	**Godfrey**: "...it was rather nice."	(Page 69/70)
	Bring up lighting on office	
Cue 8	**Wilson**: "Oh, Lord."	(Page 71)
	Blackout; when ready, bring up dim	
	lighting on station waiting-room for	
	Scene Seven	
Cue 9	**Mainwaring** helps her with her case	(Page 74)
	Crossfade to dim lighting on platform	
Cue 10	**Porter's Voice**: "Victoria train."	(Page 74)
	Fade to blackout; when ready bring up	
	dim lighting on platform and train	
	compartment for Scene Eight	
Cue 11	The train whistle blows and the train	(Page 75)
	moves off	
	Fade to spot on **Mainwaring**	
Cue 12	The sound of the train recedes into the	(Page 76)
	distance	
	Fade to blackout	

THE GODIVA AFFAIR

Property fittings required: nil

Various interior settings

To open: Full general lighting on hall and office

Cue 1	**Hancock**: "...maximum security." *Fade lighting in office*	(Page 80)
Cue 2	**Mainwaring**: "Just get in the office!" *Fade to blackout; when ready bring up* *lighting on office for Scene Two*	(Page 87)
Cue 3	**Mainwaring**: "...and arrange to meet her." *Fade to blackout; when ready bring* *up pools of light downstage left and* *downstage right for Scene Three*	(Page 90)
Cue 4	**Frazer**: "...to pay for the coffee." *Fade pools of light downstage left and* *downstage right; when ready, bring* *up pools of light on* **Cheeseman** *and* **Pike**	(Page 92)
Cue 5	**Pike**: "The tide's out tomorrow morning!" *Blackout; when ready, bring up* *lighting on tea rooms for Scene Four*	(Page 93)
Cue 6	**Mainwaring**: "You stupid boy!" *Blackout; when ready, bring up* *lighting on office for Scene Five*	(Page 98)
Cue 7	**Mainwaring**: "...is stripping down." *Crossfade to the hall*	(Page 100)
Cue 8	The girls move to the horse *Crossfade to the office*	(Page 101)
Cue 9	**Mrs Fox**: "...it's only little me!" *Bring up lighting on hall*	(Page 102)

Cue 10   **Frazer**: "You'll need a bell tent."   (Page 104)
         Blackout; when ready, bring up
         lighting on office for Scene Six

Cue 11   **Mainwaring**: "...to let sleeping dogs lie."   (Page 106)
         Blackout; when ready, bring up
         lighting on church hall for Scene
         Seven

Cue 12   **Frazer**: "...and neither will the horse."   (Page 108)
         Blackout

THE FLORAL DANCE

Property fittings required: nil

One interior

To open: Lighting on downstage area

Cue 1   **Hodges**: "Best out of three."   (Page 112)
         Blackout; when ready, bring up
         lighting on church hall for Scene Two

Cue 2   **Mainwaring** falls off the podium   (Page 120)
         Blackout

EFFECTS PLOT

THE DEADLY ATTACHMENT

Cue 1   **Mainwaring**: "...watch it."   (Page 9)
Phone rings in the office

Cue 2   **Mainwaring** follows the men out   (Page 12)
*Music for scene change; fade as Scene
Two opens*

Cue 3   **Godfrey** sits to hold the ladder   (Page 20)
Phone rings in the office

Cue 4   **Walker**: "Soggy chips."   (Page 25)
*Music for scene change; fade as Scene
Four opens*

Cue 5   **Jones** trips   (Page 30)
*The Lewis gun fires; dust and bits of
roof fall down*

MUM'S ARMY

Cue 1   **Mrs Gray**: "...it's the only way."   (Page 73)
*Steam train approaching in the
distance, growing nearer*

Cue 2   **Mainwaring**: "Go tomorrow."   (Page 74)
Train stops

Cue 3   **Mrs Gray**: "Very well—I promise."   (Page 75)
*Train whistle blows and train moves
off*

Cue 4   **Mainwaring**: Goodby, Fiona... Bye..."   (Page 76)
Dry ice, train recedes into distance

THE GODIVA AFFAIR

Cue 1 **Mainwaring**: "Just get in the office!" (Page 87)
Music for scene change

Cue 2 **Mainwaring**: "...and arrange to meet her." (Page 90)
Music for scene change

Cue 3 **Pike**: "The tide's out tomorrow morning!" (Page 93)
Music for scene change

Cue 4 **Wilson**: "Well I, er..." (Page 102)
Phone

Cue 5 **Frazer**: "You'll need a bell tent." (Page 104)
Music to cover scene change

Cue 6 **Mainwaring**: "...to let sleeping dogs lie." (Page 106)
Music to cover scene change

Cue 7 **Mainwaring**: "...do the best you can, (Page 107)
Godfrey."
Sound of a band and crowds cheering

Cue 8 **Jones**: "...just tell me what's the matter." (Page 107)
Music gets louder

THE FLORAL DANCE

No cues

VISIT THE
SAMUEL FRENCH
BOOKSHOP
AT THE
ROYAL COURT THEATRE

Browse plays and theatre books, get expert advice and enjoy a coffee

Samuel French Bookshop
Royal Court Theatre
Sloane Square
London
SW1W 8AS
020 7565 5024

Shop from thousands of titles on our website

 samuelfrench.co.uk

 samuelfrenchltd

 samuel french uk